Gender, Power and Political Speech

Deborah Cameron • Sylvia Shaw

Gender, Power and Political Speech

Women and Language in the 2015 UK General Election

palgrave
macmillan

Deborah Cameron
Worcester College
University of Oxford
Oxford, United Kingdom

Sylvia Shaw
Media Department
Middlesex University
London, United Kingdom

ISBN 978-1-137-58751-0   ISBN 978-1-137-58752-7   (eBook)
DOI 10.1057/978-1-137-58752-7

Library of Congress Control Number: 2016935190

Printed on acid-free paper

This Palgrave Macmillan imprint is published by Springer Nature
The registered company is Macmillan Publishers Ltd. London

ACKNOWLEDGEMENTS

We would like to thank Mariam Kauser, for help with the first stages of transcribing the televised debates, and Rob Heard. We are also grateful to Karen Adams, Charlie Beckett, and John Wilson for sharing early versions of their publications.

CONTENTS

LIST OF FIGURES

CHAPTER 1

A Different Voice?

Abstract This chapter sets out the questions to be addressed in the book as a whole. It introduces the notion of women's 'different voice' as both a linguistic and a sociopolitical construct, and reviews research dealing with gender as an influence on verbal behaviour in political and other public or institutional settings. It then outlines the context and main events of the 2015 General Election campaign in the UK, including the two televised leaders' debates which are at the centre of this book's case study of female political leaders' speech. The chapter ends with a brief account of the case study approach, and summarizes the aims and methods of the present study.

Keywords Different voice • General Election • Language ideology • Male dominance • UK politics • Women in politics

INTRODUCTION

In September 2015, as we were finishing this book, two men—Jeremy Corbyn and Tom Watson—were elected to serve as leader and deputy leader of Britain's Labour Party. Both positions had been contested by women, and the fact that a man was preferred in each case divided opinion among Labour supporters. One view was that the gender of a leader

© The Editor(s) (if applicable) and The Author(s) 2016
D. Cameron, S. Shaw, *Gender, Power and Political Speech*,
DOI 10.1057/978-1-137-58752-7_1

matters less than his or her politics: in this case, the socialist policies advocated by the winning candidate would do more to advance the interests of most women than the less radical policies favoured by his two female rivals. An opposing view, however, was that gender is important in its own right: the presence of women in leadership roles makes a difference both to the content and to the conduct of politics. In support of this argument, Yvonne Roberts (2015) cited the example of the recent General Election campaign, in which three female party leaders had featured prominently:

> Nicola Sturgeon for the SNP [Scottish National Party] and Leanne Wood for Plaid Cymru [the Party of Wales] changed the debate not just because of what they said, but *how* they said it and the way in which they related to each other and the electorate – a visibly different kind of politics.

The sentence just quoted contains two related propositions which are central to our concerns in this book: first, that women, by virtue of their gender, offer a 'different kind of politics'; and second, that this difference is inextricably linked to the way women use language in political contexts—not just *what* they say, the political content, but *how* they say it, the style of interaction. This is not a novel observation: in fact, over the past two decades, it has become a cliché of British political journalism. After the 1997 General Election, when the landslide victory of Tony Blair's 'New' Labour party brought what was then a record number of women—119—into Parliament, commentators suggested approvingly that their presence would make the House of Commons debating chamber 'less of a bear-garden'. Similar sentiments were expressed by some of the new women MPs (Members of Parliament) themselves. Julia Drown explained that 'women are more co-operative in the way they work. They're not so into scoring points, and more interested in hearing different points of view', while her colleague Gisela Stuart noted that 'what [women] will do is make politics more relevant to people's lives: democracy is about consensus rather than imposing will' (Cameron 1997). These comments are expressions of what we will refer to as the 'different voice' ideology of gender, language, and politics. They suggest that women's distinctive political contribution is a way of doing things—and saying things—that eschews aggression and point-scoring in favour of cooperation and consensus, making politics more civilized, more modern, and more human.

As language and gender researchers, we are interested in the political speech of women—both what it is, and what it is believed to be. But those two things are not always easy to disentangle. For many commentators on women's 'different voice', including not only journalists and politicians but also academic researchers outside the field of language and gender studies, 'voice' is a metaphor for a whole cluster of distinctive qualities and concerns women are said to bring into the political arena. In many studies, the main focus of attention is not linguistic style so much as political substance: the question is how women's presence as 'critical actors' in institutions (Childs and Krook 2009) helps to shape political agendas or increase the visibility of issues in which women have a particular stake (Chaney 2012; Mackay 2004). It is often claimed that women also have a 'different voice' in the more narrowly linguistic sense, but most commonly, the basis for this assertion is the accounts women give of their linguistic behaviour when they are talking more generally about their difference from men. For example, when the British researcher Sarah Childs (2004) conducted in-depth interviews with twenty-three Labour women MPs who had entered the House of Commons in 1997, almost two thirds of them expressed the belief that women have a different approach to politics, and language was mentioned repeatedly as one of the key markers of the difference. Women were said to prefer a 'less combative and aggressive style', with 'less standing up and shouting on the floor of the House', and more collaborating with others behind the scenes. They were also described as communicating in a more personal and less abstruse way, without using political 'babble [and] jargon', and without adopting such undesirable male practices as making cutting remarks while others were speaking, unnecessarily repeating others' points, or talking just for the sake of talking (Childs 2004: 5, 6). The women accorded positive value to the style of speech they described, but they also complained that it was viewed as less legitimate and less effective than the traditional 'male' style. One interviewee had been told by a Whip (an enforcer of party discipline) that she should be more combative, while another believed that the female preference for less jargon and more everyday English was regarded by others as 'naïve'.

These observations point to a paradox. Many or most public comments on women's different way of speaking either say or imply that it is preferable to men's. No journalist or politician, of either sex or any party allegiance, ever says: 'what we really need in politics is less constructive dialogue and more shouting, jeering and hurling accusations'. Yet in practice, women—the group which supposedly embodies all the virtues people say they want to see more of in politics (and none of the vices they say they want to see less of)—remain marginalized, a minority at all levels, and a vanishingly small minority in positions of political leadership. Is all this talk about the virtues of women's style just lip service? Does it function as a form of sexism in its own right, a way of keeping women in their subordinate place? What does it mean, concretely, to say that women as a group speak a different political language, and how far do descriptions of that language, such as the ones quoted above, correspond to women's actual behaviour in political settings?

Those questions will be explored in the following chapters, where we examine the status and workings of the 'different voice' ideology in contemporary democratic politics, using the UK General Election of 2015 (hereafter 'GE2015') as a case study. At the heart of our case study is an empirical question, which we address in Chap. 2: how did male and female politicians actually use language in key public speech events during the election campaign? Does an analysis of their discourse support the belief that women political leaders have a 'different voice', and if so, how is the difference best described? In addition, though, we are interested in the way the existence of the 'different voice' ideology (whether or not it is empirically well founded in linguistic terms) affects the public perception of female politicians and the terms on which they participate in public discourse. With that in mind, in Chap. 3, we analyse the way the women party leaders—and more specifically, their styles of speaking—were represented in media coverage of GE2015. We compare the representation of their language use with the findings of our own analysis, and consider how far the reception of their speech was influenced by the 'different voice' ideology.

Before we turn to our case study, however, there are a number of preliminaries to be dealt with. Since not all readers will have followed GE2015, later on in this chapter we provide a brief narrative of the campaign, along with other background information that is needed to contextualize our case study. We also give a general account of our approach and the methods we have chosen to employ. First, though, we explore the wider intellectual context in which the questions we propose to investigate are located, relating our own study to previous work in a number of academic disciplines addressing questions about (in various combinations) gender, language, and politics.

GENDER AND SPEECH STYLE: IDEOLOGY AND PRACTICE

When we use the phrase '"different voice" *ideology*', we are placing the belief that women have a distinctive style of communication in the category of what anthropologists and linguists call *language ideologies*—'sets of beliefs about language articulated by the users as a rationalization or justification of perceived language structure and use' (Silverstein 1979: 193, 194). The implication of the term *ideology* is not necessarily that the belief in question distorts or misrepresents reality. There are types of language ideology, such as origin myths in which human language is created by a god or other supernatural being, to which positivist notions of truth are entirely irrelevant. Other language ideological beliefs may be close to, or at least not incompatible with, scientific accounts of the phenomenon they concern. However, language ideologies are representations which *idealize* their object, rendering the actual complexity of linguistic practice more intelligible through simplification, generalization, and stereotyping. They are typically also, as Silverstein says, *rationalizations*, attempts to explain what people perceive as significant facts about language use in a way that is consonant with their more general beliefs about the world. Language ideologies thus come with what Judith Irvine (1989: 255) describes as a 'loading of moral and political interests'.

The relationship between language and gender is a common subject for these morally and politically loaded rationalizations. Exactly what language users believe about it can vary considerably across cultures and historical periods (Cameron 2007), but as Sherzer (1987) points out, a community's understanding of the speech of men and women is invariably related to its understanding of the qualities and proper social roles of men and women themselves. Gender differences in language use are not treated as arbitrary and superficial, but are taken to index deeper differences in ways of thinking, feeling, and relating to others.

As that last statement suggests, most ideologies of language and gender, past as well as present, centre on the belief that women use language in a different way from men. What we mean when we refer to the 'different voice' ideology, however, is something more specific than just 'a belief that men and women are different'. In the form we consider it here, the 'different voice' ideology is a product of the late twentieth century. While it has clear continuities with earlier representations of gender differences in language use, it is also clearly indebted to the ideas and political aspirations of the late twentieth-century feminist movement, and it is not only a common-sense or 'folk' ideology, but also one which has been elaborated in influential academic texts.

The phrase 'different voice' alludes to one of those texts, the US psychologist Carol Gilligan's book *In a Different Voice* (Gilligan 1982). Like the political scientists mentioned earlier, Gilligan does not treat women's 'different voice' as an exclusively linguistic phenomenon: though she does touch on language, the real subject of her book is gender differences in moral decision-making, and its thesis is that men tend to think of morality in terms of respecting individual rights and freedoms, whereas women tend to be more concerned with fulfilling obligations and meeting others' needs. However, this notion of gender difference, and the oppositions which constitute it (e.g. autonomy/interdependence, rights/needs, justice/care), has influenced work that deals more specifically with language. It is echoed, for instance, in the work of the linguist Deborah Tannen (1990; 1994), a central figure in the development of what is sometimes called the 'difference' or 'two cultures' model of male and female communication styles. Tannen's argument is that boys and girls learn differing norms of interaction in the same-sex peer groups, which are at the centre of children's social lives. Boys, whose peer groups are typically large and hierarchically organized, learn to interact in ways that foreground conflict and competition for status. Girls, whose peer groups are smaller and organized in looser, more egalitarian ways, learn to interact in ways that foreground cooperation, mutual support, and the avoidance or smoothing over of conflicts. These norms, acquired in childhood, are carried over into adult life, where they are liable to cause problems of miscommunication in relationships between men and women.

The book in which Tannen presented this account to a non-specialist audience, *You Just Don't Understand* (Tannen 1990), was an international bestseller; it was soon followed by an even more successful popular book, John Grey's *Men are from Mars, Women are from Venus* (1992), which argued that men talk to accomplish tasks, solve problems, and gain status, whereas women talk to make connections with others, share experiences, and express their feelings. By the first decade of the twenty-first century, these claims had been woven into a more general account of male–female differences which related them to the structure and functioning of male and female brains (e.g. Baron-Cohen 2003). In these popularized forms, the 'different voice' ideology has become familiar to a mass audience: for many people, it has attained the status of self-evident common sense. It is this that enables writers like Yvonne Roberts to assert that the female political leaders who took part in GE2015 'changed the debate not only because of what they said but *how* they said it', without needing to elaborate on what she means by 'how they said it'. She can rely on readers' familiarity with widely circulated propositions about linguistic differences between men and women—for instance, that women prefer cooperative and supportive interaction to aggressive argument, and are less interested in point-scoring and self-promotion than in displaying empathy and building rapport. This is probably the dominant 'folk' ideology of language and gender in contemporary western societies. How, though, does it relate to the findings of empirical research focusing not on ideology but on practice, the concrete details of male and female verbal behaviour?

The popularity of the 'two cultures' model in its 'folk' versions has never been matched by the level of support for it among language and gender scholars, many of whom have criticized it on both theoretical and empirical grounds (e.g. Cameron 2007; Goodwin 2006; Uchida 1998). In her book *The Hidden Life of Girls*, an ethnographic study of a preadolescent girls' peer group, Marjorie Goodwin is critical both of the 'dualistic thinking' that underpins the approach and the strength of the evidence presented to support its empirical claims about linguistic and other behaviour, noting that 'much of the work... that argues for "a different voice" among females has investigated middle-class Euro-American groups and has been conducted through interviews rather than extensive fieldwork' (Goodwin 2006: 19). Her own findings do not support Tannen's account of language use in girls' peer groups; there is also research which challenges some of the familiar generalizations about boys (e.g. Way 2013). Since the 1990s, criticisms of what Goodwin calls 'dualistic thinking', together with the emergence of new research evidence which challenges it, have prompted a general shift away from the assumption that the goal of language and gender research is to produce broad generalizations about the differences between male and female speakers. Instead, researchers have adopted the principle of 'looking locally', examining the specific ways in which gender influences language use in particular contexts and 'communities of practice' (Eckert and McConnell-Ginet 1992). This entails paying attention to similarities as well as differences between men and women, and to differences within each gender group as well as differences between the two. In this newer paradigm, there has been a retreat from 'grand narratives' of male–female difference, including not only the 'two cultures' narrative favoured by Tannen, but also the 'dominance' narrative that explains gendered linguistic behaviour in terms of structural social inequality between men and women.

However, some scholars have asked whether the recent emphasis on 'looking locally' has caused feminist researchers to lose sight of the bigger picture. The anthropologist Susan Phillips (2003: 259, 260) asserts:

> While a great deal was gained by the new feminist conceptualizing of women as intersections of various aspects of social identity, a great deal was lost too. The rhetorical force of the focus on the universal key problem of a very broad male power over women...was obscured.

If there is one linguistic phenomenon that might plausibly be described as a 'universal key problem of...male power over women', it must surely be the tendency for women to be excluded, marginalized, or under-represented relative to men in the forums and genres where speech is most authoritative, influential, and culturally prestigious. Unlike the claim that women have a universal preference for a particular *style* of speaking, to which there are many counter-examples, the claim that men occupy a disproportionate share of the floor in public settings is supported by research evidence from a wide range of different societies and institutional settings.

In the case which is most directly relevant to our concerns in this book, political speech in modern democracies, the evidence of male dominance is overwhelming. A recent overview, presented by Christopher Karpowitz and Tali Mendelberg in their book *The Silent Sex* (2014), shows that at every level of political discussion and democratic decision-making, from the town meeting to the national legislature, women are typically a minority of those who speak, even when they are a majority of those present. Men speak more frequently and for longer than women; they more often take leadership roles in formal settings, and are more likely to be the speakers whose contributions are most influential, in the sense that others take them up and refer to them in subsequent discussion. This means that increasing women's 'descriptive' representation (i.e. their numbers in an institution) does not necessarily produce an improvement in their 'substantive' representation (i.e. the extent to which their views actually influence the decision-making process). Karpowitz and Mendelberg even cite studies which have found the opposite effect—men becoming more verbally dominant as women's numbers increase (Kathlene 1994).

Much of *The Silent Sex* is devoted to reporting the research in which Karpowitz and Mendelberg sought to investigate the effect of two variables on women's participation in one type of political discourse (small group deliberation): the gender composition of the group and its decision-making procedure. Their main study (a concise report of which appears as Karpowitz et al. 2012) used an experimental design that allowed them to manipulate these variables. Subjects were assigned to groups of five, constructed to represent every possible male–female ratio, and instructed to deliberate on a question about the fairest way of allocating resources, before collectively deciding which option they preferred (they had been briefed on the options before the discussion). Some groups were told to decide by majority vote, while others were told that their choice had to be unanimous. The researchers then computed the amount and proportion of speaking time taken by each participant, and by men and women as groups. They wanted to know whether deviations from the 'ideal', equal distribution (each individual taking one fifth of the time, and thus each gender group contributing in proportion to its 'descriptive' representation) were greater under some conditions than others.

In fact, they found that women got less than their fair share of the speaking time under almost all conditions. In mixed groups they only contributed as much speech as their numbers entitled them to when they were not merely a majority but a 'super-majority', outnumbering men 4:1. Under all other conditions they took less than their share, and the more they were outnumbered by men, the larger the imbalance was. Men, by contrast, were never disadvantaged by being numerically in the minority. Even lone 'token' men in otherwise all-female groups took at least the 20 % share of the floor that they were notionally entitled to. The procedure a group used to make decisions had some effect: female minorities in unanimous decision-making groups got more speaking time than their counterparts who had been assigned to majority voting groups. If women were in the majority, however, they did better in groups that used majority voting. Unanimous decision-making always benefited the minority (as you might logically expect: if everyone has to agree, then everyone also has to speak). But whereas women used this benefit to claim as much time as they were entitled to, men used it to claim more than their numbers warranted. Nor were these findings just an artefact of the experimental conditions. When Karpowitz and Mendelberg repeated the analysis using naturally occurring data from a real-world setting (the deliberations of US school boards, one type of public body on which women are reasonably well represented), they found broadly the same pattern.

What explains the gender imbalance? Karpowitz and Mendelberg suggest that the root cause of it is the gender norm which associates authority with maleness. This gives men a stronger sense than women of their entitlement to exercise authority, which in the context of politics requires the oral, public expression of one's views. Women are both less convinced that their views are worth hearing and less confident in their public speaking abilities—perceptions which contribute not only to their relative silence in mixed-sex forums, but also to their under-representation in the institutions where those interactions are most consequential. In the case of political institutions, Fox and Lawless (2011: 59) report that women are significantly less likely to seek office than male peers whose qualifications are objectively no better than theirs. In addition to lacking confidence in their own ability to speak with authority, women may actively avoid speaking out in public because of the risk that engaging in normatively 'masculine' behaviour will have adverse social consequences. Research confirms what many women have learnt from experience—that overt displays of authority by women prompt others to judge them negatively on measures of both femininity and likeability (Rudman 1998; Rudman and Fairchild 2004).

The account just given of the 'authority gap' between men and women does not centre on the issue of gender differences in communicative style. However, Karpowitz and Mendelberg argue that those differences are also a factor contributing to the pattern of male dominance: the norms of mixed-sex political discourse do not suit women's preference for a collaborative, supportive, and egalitarian form of interaction, but rather emphasize forms of competition and conflict which women actively dislike. In support of this argument, they note that in their own study, women spoke far more in all-female groups ('enclaves' where they could conduct discussions largely on their own terms) than in mixed groups, and that women in mixed groups spoke more when they received encouragement and agreement from others, whereas they spoke less when their contributions were met with disagreement, criticism, or dismissal. Citing research which has found men to be more resilient than women in the face of negative feedback, the researchers speculate that women need more support than men to facilitate their participation in political discussions, and conversely that they are more easily silenced by the absence of support.

The subjects who participated in Karpowitz and Mendelberg's research were not politicians, and (with the exception of the school board members in the naturalistic part of the study) most did not have extensive experience of the kind of discussion they were being asked to engage in. The question arises, then, of whether the factors that were associated with men's dominance in the experimental study, such as women's relative lack of confidence and their preference for a certain style of interaction, become less significant in contexts where women have more experience of the relevant linguistic norms. Earlier in this chapter we discussed one kind of evidence bearing on this question, namely interviews in which women MPs claimed to behave differently from men. Many of the women interviewed by Childs (2004) reported reluctance to adopt the adversarial linguistic norms of the institution, and some also reported feeling insecure about their competence in certain forms of adversarial speech. But while these self-reports are, as Childs points out, data, they are not (as she also acknowledges) conclusive evidence that women MPs actually do behave differently from men. In the terms we introduced above, they are evidence about language ideology, not linguistic practice. Studies of gender and linguistic practice in institutional settings tell a more complicated story: it is neither a case of women using a totally different style from men, nor a case of women's behaviour being indistinguishable in every respect from that of their male colleagues.

Gender and Linguistic Practice in Institutional Settings

A number of researchers have studied the linguistic behaviour of women who have entered 'masculinist' institutions—workplaces, institutions, or professions which historically excluded women, and where women continue to be outnumbered and outranked by men. Cases which have been studied in some detail include the police service (McElhinny 1995), the Anglican priesthood (Walsh 2001), and the British House of Commons (Shaw 2000). On balance, the findings of this research suggest that what influences speech style most is not the gender of the speaker so much as the culture of the institution: women entering male-dominated occupations and institutions most often adopt the style of speaking which is already established as the institutional norm. (The same appears to be true of men in female-dominated professions such as nursing (McDowell 2015)).

The anthropologist Bonnie McElhinny studied linguistic practice in the Pittsburgh police department (1995), a historically male-dominated institution which had recently recruited a significant number of officers from under-represented groups, including women. She observed that female police officers fairly quickly adopted the prevailing style of speaking, which was characterized among other things by a relative absence of markers of affect such as pitch variation and smiling. Frequent smiling and the use of a wide pitch range are culturally coded as 'feminine' linguistic characteristics, so in a sense what the women were doing was accommodating to a 'masculine' norm. However, in interviews, they generally rejected that description, saying that they did not speak like men, but like police officers. The low-affect style was simply the most appropriate one for the demands of the job, which required officers to project a calm authority in volatile and potentially dangerous situations. As McElhinny notes, though, assumptions about how policing should be done, and what qualities it requires, are inevitably shaped by its history as a male occupation. To put it another way, gender is not just a characteristic of individual persons, but also a property of institutions. Similarly, the linguist Janet Holmes, who directed a seven-year study of male and female managers' speech in twenty-two different organizations in New Zealand, uses the concept of a 'gendered workplace' (Holmes 2006: 10–12). In this study, both male and female managers were found to use a wide range of styles, from the extremely directive to the highly collaborative; what explained their behaviour was not their own gender, but rather the 'masculine' or 'feminine' ethos of the organization in which they worked.

The point that institutions are gendered, and that their norms, rules, and procedures may both reflect and reproduce gender inequality, has also been made by feminist scholars about democratic political institutions (see, e.g., Krook and Mackay 2011). As we have already seen, it is frequently argued that the adversarial linguistic norms which prevail in many political settings contribute to the continuing under-representation of women, both descriptive (insofar as they deter women from seeking office) and substantive (insofar as they prevent women who have entered political institutions from participating fully in the discourse of those institutions). However, the evidence cited so far for that view has been based on either self-report data from interviews or somewhat speculative interpretations of quantitative experimental findings. By contrast, Sylvia Shaw (2006) both interviewed women MPs and analysed their speech in a sample of debates, from which she concluded that there was a gap between their perceptions (which were similar to those reported by Childs (2004)) and their actual performance in the debating chamber. Shaw found no evidence that women's style of debate differed significantly from men's. What she did observe was another kind of gender difference: women's participation in debates was constrained in ways that men's was not.

One constraint women faced was men's practice of barracking women speakers with a stream of overtly sexist comments. As well as affecting their performance when it happened, anticipation of this kind of response made women less willing to put themselves in the firing line by claiming the floor. Another factor which limited their participation (one we discuss more fully in Chap. 2) was their own reluctance to engage in rule-breaking, a common practice in the House of Commons, and one which is regarded by insiders as one of the marks of a skilful and effective speaker. In this and other male-dominated public institutions, a recurring problem for women is, precisely, that they are not automatically accorded the status and privileges of insiders, but are rather seen and treated in a way that makes them feel like 'interlopers'. They may be members of the same community of practice, but they do not participate on equal terms with men. And if one thing that makes the terms of participation unequal is overt sexism (including the kind of extreme resistance to women's public speech whose past and present manifestations have been discussed by Mary Beard (2014)), another, perhaps less obvious constraint on women is the 'different voice' ideology itself.

The potentially negative consequences for women of the belief that they are and should be different are highlighted in Clare Walsh's account of women's experiences in the Anglican priesthood (Walsh 2001), where the expectation that women would speak and act in a different way from men became both a condition for their acceptance as members of the institution and a factor limiting the contribution they were able to make to it. Even more than the MPs discussed above, the women priests Walsh interviewed were themselves committed to the idea of women's difference. One of the arguments they had used during the long and bitter campaign for women's ordination was that women would bring something to the priesthood which men could not. This 'something' was conceptualized in a way reminiscent of Carol Gilligan's claims: women were said to have a particular commitment to the ideals of service and care for others, and to fostering more egalitarian relationships within the Church. Ultimately, their case for admission was accepted; once ordained, however, they often found themselves being channelled into what were seen as gender-appropriate areas of work, such as counselling bereaved or troubled parishioners, while the parts of the job that involved public visibility and leadership, like preaching or organizing parish activities, were assigned to men. Some explained that what they resented was not being assigned 'low-status' tasks, since they disputed the definition of status that implied; but they had wanted their distinctive qualities as women to influence the whole range of the Church's activities, and were dismayed to be confined to a narrowly circumscribed area in which many issues that were important to them were beyond their power to affect.

Walsh's work exemplifies what has sometimes been called a 'critical difference' view of language and gender: it does not axiomatically reject the claim that women have a 'different voice', but seeks to avoid the essentialism and 'dualistic thinking' for which less critical accounts have been criticized. It does not suggest that women's stylistic preferences are 'natural' or that all women exhibit them in all contexts; it also takes on board the point that stylistic differences, where they exist, do not arise in a social vacuum. The gendered peer group norms described by Tannen, for instance, are not just arbitrarily different, but also appear to be preparing boys and girls for a traditional division of roles, where males compete with one another in the public sphere, while women perform caring and emotional labour in the private domestic sphere. Simply saying that the styles should be treated as 'different but equal' overlooks the fact that the roles for which they equip speakers are constitutive of a social hierarchy in which women are subordinate to men. As Walsh points out, what the Anglican Church did in response to the ordination of women was create its own internal version of the public/private divide, through which the same gender hierarchy was reproduced. However, she argues (as does Baxter (2010) from a feminist post-structuralist perspective) that women's 'different voice' should not be seen only as a mark of subordinate status within a hierarchical system. The ways of speaking associated with women do have value, and they also have the potential to be exploited strategically in pursuit of women's own political objectives.

This is illustrated by another case Walsh discusses, that of the Northern Ireland Women's Coalition (NIWC), a women's political organization organized on non-sectarian lines and feminist political principles, which managed to win representation at the peace talks that produced the Good Friday Agreement and initiated the Northern Ireland peace process. The NIWC consciously set out to be a civilizing influence, in a context where the incivility of most political discourse could hardly be overstated. The coalition's representatives emphasized, and modelled, such 'female' linguistic strategies as resisting provocation, listening to opponents' arguments, and being willing to compromise. As a result, Walsh argues, the women had more influence in the peace negotiations and the drafting of the Agreement than they are generally given credit for. In her view, both they and the women priests often used a language of moderation and consensus to disguise what were actually quite radical political aims. But while she believes that this can be an effective strategy, she is also aware that what makes it necessary is the fact that women have to operate in conditions of institutionalized inequality.

DIFFERENCE, INEQUALITY, AND THE PARADOX OF FEMALE LEADERSHIP

Academic researchers who believe it is legitimate to talk about male and female speech styles have tended to adopt (at least overtly) the position that these styles are 'different but equal'. What produces gender inequality is not difference in and of itself, but the fact that male and female ways of speaking are not accorded equal value, so that women in public settings are forced to accommodate to male norms in order to be (or be judged as) effective. However, as we pointed out at the beginning of this chapter, 'folk' versions of the 'different voice' ideology often imply a preference for female styles, and sometimes describe male styles in ways that are difficult to interpret as anything but disparaging. Julia Drown's claim that women 'are not so into scoring points, and more interested in hearing different points of view', for instance, does not look much like an assertion that the two styles have equal value.

The idea, stated or implied, that women are actually *better* communicators than men is an important element in the variant of the 'different voice' ideology that Deborah Cameron (2007) labels 'the myth of Mars and Venus'. And while the prototypical subject of 'Mars and Venus' discourse is intimate relationships between men and women, there are also examples of it being used in political contexts. In 2006, for instance, when the outgoing Labour Prime Minister Tony Blair predicted that his successor Gordon Brown would not only win the next election, he would knock out his Conservative opponent David Cameron with 'a big clunking fist', the political journalist Andrew Rawnsley (2006) commented that it would not be good for Labour if voters believed that 'Gordon Brown is from Mars, David Cameron is from Venus'. Both in politics and in business, an effective leader is no longer imagined as an aggressive, ruthless, hyper-competitive individualist; the 'modern' ideal of leadership emphasizes 'people skills' such as teamwork and motivation, which call for the Venusian virtues of cooperation, empathy, and openness (Chamorro-Premuzic 2013).

Yet as we noted earlier, there is a paradox here: this modern, Venusian leader is still more likely to be male than female. Cameron (2003: 463) argues that the main beneficiaries of the shift towards a more 'Venusian' ideal of leadership have not been the prototypical Venusians, women, but rather men like Tony Blair, Bill Clinton, and Barack Obama, whose communication styles encompass *both* traditionally 'masculine' qualities (such as the ability to project authority and score points in adversarial exchanges) *and* the 'feminine' capacity to forge connections with others and express emotion in a way that feels 'sincere' and 'authentic'. Partly this may be because men are given extra credit for showing any interpersonal skills at all, whereas women's interpersonal skills are considered 'natural'. But it may also be because women leaders have a problem which is harder to solve, and which takes us back to the points made earlier about the perception of authority as normatively male. On the one hand, that perception will tend to prompt doubts about whether a woman who aspires to leadership possesses the necessary authority; on the other, a woman who displays authority will often be judged as both unfeminine and unlikeable, which undermines her perceived ability to connect with people on a personal level. The demand for leaders who are both authoritative and likeable is particularly difficult for women to meet: however they behave, they are obliged to walk, as Janet Holmes (2006: 35) puts it, 'a tightrope of impression management'.

Our case study of GE2015 is intended to contribute to the wider debates on gender, language, and politics which this section has discussed by focusing on the linguistic performances, in two high-profile and highly adversarial speech events (televised election debates), of three women who walked this metaphorical tightrope: Natalie Bennett, who led the Green Party; Nicola Sturgeon, the leader of the Scottish National Party (SNP); and Leanne Wood, leader of Plaid Cymru. The 2015 campaign was the first in British history in which a group of women played such a prominent role. As such, it offers an opportunity to explore some of the claims that have been made about women as political speakers and political leaders. In a context where party leaders of both sexes addressed the same audience, on the same topics and under the same institutional conditions, were there identifiable stylistic differences between the men and the women? If so, were these in line with the claim that women prefer a less adversarial, more collaborative style of speech? How similar or different were the women themselves? Where they differed, was that related to their ways of per-forming gender, or did it have more to do with individual differences in temperament, experience, or skill? Did women participate in the debates on equal terms with men? Were they judged by the same criteria, and was the 'different voice' ideology a factor in the way their performances were received? How did they balance the competing demands for authority and likeability? Were they able to exploit their status as women strategically, or was their performance, in Clare Walsh's words, 'fractured by competing and often contradictory norms and expectations' (Walsh 2001: 201)?

Before those questions can be considered, though, it is necessary to provide some background information about the debates, the politicians who participated in them, and the context in which they took place.

THE 2015 UK GENERAL ELECTION CAMPAIGN

As the name suggests, a 'General' election in the UK is an election in which all Parliamentary seats are contested simultaneously. (As the law now stands, this normally happens every five years.) British Parliamentary elections use a 'first-past-the-post' system rather than any form of pro-portional representation: the candidate who is elected to represent a constituency in Parliament is the one for whom most votes are cast by electors registered in that constituency. The party that wins most seats through this system is typically invited to form a government, though if it does not have an overall majority in the House of Commons, it may have to negotiate with other parties for their support, or enter into a coalition.

In recent times this has been a relatively rare occurrence. Most General Elections since 1945 have essentially been two-way contests between the Conservative and Labour parties. The third party, the Liberal Democrats (formerly Liberals), has usually had a smaller but still non-negligible pres-ence in the House of Commons, while other parties (mostly those that only contest seats in Scotland, Wales, or Northern Ireland) have generally been more marginal in terms of numbers. 'Fringe' parties, such as the racist British National Party and the joke Monster Raving Loony Party, have regularly contested seats in General Elections (and did so again in 2015), but never successfully; the Green Party, though reasonably suc-cessful in local council elections, has only ever won one Parliamentary seat. The UK Independence Party (UKIP) is a relative newcomer, whose main electoral successes to date have been in European elections: its leader

Nigel Farage gained his political experience as an MEP (Member of the European Parliament) rather than in any UK-based institution.[1]

The 2010 General Election was a case where neither the Conservatives nor Labour won an overall majority. The eventual result was a Conservative–Liberal Democrat coalition government, in which the Conservative leader David Cameron served as Prime Minister and the Liberal Democrat leader Nick Clegg as his deputy. As the 2015 election approached, many political commentators and pollsters believed it would be another close race which no party would win outright. It was noted, for instance, that Labour's traditional dominance in Scotland was under threat from the SNP, which had gained supporters following the 2014 referendum on Scottish independence, while the Conservatives faced a challenge from UKIP, which had acquired two seats in the House of Commons after sitting Conservative MPs defected, and then successfully fought by-elections as UKIP candidates.

These details are relevant because they help to explain the prominence of the three women our case study focuses on—a prominence they achieved mainly because of their inclusion in the televised leaders' debates, which were the campaign's most important media events. It was not a foregone conclusion that they would participate: the rules governing election broadcasting do not require that equal representation be given to every political party. The parties the women led were peripheral rather than central to the electoral politics of the UK as a whole (though the two nationalist parties played an important role in their own territories, Scotland and Wales): none of them held more than a handful of Parliamentary seats before the General Election (though the SNP would hold a much more significant number after it).[2] Only one of the women, Bennett, was actually a candidate in the election, and she was contesting a safe Labour seat that she had no realistic chance of winning. In many ways, then, it is remarkable that any of them, let alone all of them, ended up participating in the debates

---

[1] For readers unfamiliar with British politics, it should be explained that UKIP opposes the UK's membership of the European Union (EU), and has sought representation in European institutions in order to pursue its anti-EU agenda from the inside. In UK national politics it stands not only for opposition to the EU, but also for opposition to immigration—the cause which is most strongly associated with right-wing populism in Britain.

[2] Before the campaign the SNP held six seats in the House of Commons, Plaid Cymru three and the Greens one. In the 2015 election Plaid and the Greens maintained their position, while the SNP's representation rose to fifty-six seats.

alongside the two leaders of the outgoing coalition government and the Labour Leader of the Opposition.

Televised leaders' debates were themselves a recent innovation in British General Election campaigns, taking place for the first time in 2010. On that occasion there were three debates, and none of the smaller parties took part in any of them: the participants were the leaders of the three largest parties, the Conservatives, Labour, and the Liberal Democrats. Initially, the broadcasters proposed another series of three debates for 2015; they also suggested that one of them should be a head-to-head debate between the Conservative and Labour leaders, David Cameron and Ed Miliband. However, Cameron declined to cooperate with this plan, refusing to debate Miliband one-to-one and insisting that he would only participate in one debate of any kind. He also expressed a preference for an inclusive line-up, thus giving powerful support to the demands for representation which smaller parties (UKIP, the Greens, and those based outside England) were making. In the event, only the Northern Irish parties were excluded. It was agreed that there would be two debates, one broadcast on the main commercial channel, ITV, and the other on the BBC two weeks later. The first would feature seven party leaders (Cameron, Clegg, Miliband, Farage, Sturgeon, Bennett, and Wood). The second, since Cameron had refused to take part in it, would exclude both the leaders of the coalition parties, and be billed as a 'challengers' debate' featuring the other five party leaders. (The format of the two debates is described more fully in Chap. 2.) Together, the debates drew substantial audiences of sixteen million viewers (Beckett 2015).

The debates were not the only significant broadcasts of the campaign: apart from the short election broadcasts produced by the parties themselves, there were also in-depth interviews with the party leaders on national radio and TV, a special edition of the political panel show *Question Time* featuring Cameron, Miliband, and Clegg, and—in lieu of the head-to-head debate Cameron had vetoed—a programme entitled *Cameron and Miliband: The Battle for Number 10*, in which the two men were separately interviewed and questioned by a studio audience. Most of the highest-profile media slots went to the leaders of the main parties, but the other leaders who took part in the debates also received a level of national attention which none of them (except perhaps Farage) could otherwise have counted on. The debates were not only important occasions in themselves, they were also the key which unlocked other opportunities for leaders to raise their public profiles. For the three women, particularly the previously little-known Bennett and Wood, it was their inclusion in the debates that made them into national figures, and enabled them to occupy a position which no group of female politicians had ever occupied in a UK General Election campaign before: they joined a select group of political leaders whose public utterances dominated the campaign and the media reporting of the campaign. In the case of the second debate, from which Cameron and Clegg were absent, the presence of the three women produced the novel spectacle of a high-profile national political event where female speakers outnumbered male ones.

Who were these women? All of them had risen to positions of political leadership, but of different kinds and by different routes. Two of them, Sturgeon and Wood, served as elected representatives in the devolved legislative assemblies of Scotland and Wales. Sturgeon had most experience of executive power: following the 2014 referendum on Scottish independence (which ended with a narrow victory for the 'no' camp), she had succeeded Alex Salmond as First Minister of Scotland. She had previously been his deputy, and had also held other ministerial positions. Leanne Wood's Plaid Cymru was a smaller party (and not the ruling party) within a smaller legislative assembly which had fewer devolved powers; she, therefore, had less experience of wielding power and a lower public profile than Sturgeon. Natalie Bennett was the least politically experienced of the three: an Australian former journalist, she had never been a member of any legislative body. Politically, all three stood to the left of the Labour party, and opposed the deficit reduction or 'austerity' policies to which, in some form or other, all the other parties were committed. This shared political position was the basis for an alliance among the women: while they did not exactly operate as a bloc in the debates (see our analysis in Chap. 2), they did maintain a united front, arguing with the men rather than with each other. At the end of the second debate, they engaged in a group hug, which became one of the iconic images of the campaign.

Voting took place on 7 May 2015, and by the next day, it was clear that the pollsters who had predicted a close race with no outright winner had been wrong. The Conservatives won a small overall majority with 331 seats. Labour had 232. The SNP took fifty-six of the fifty-nine Scottish constituencies (many of them previously held by Labour), and since the Liberal Democrat vote collapsed, leaving the party with only eight seats where it had previously had fifty-seven, the SNP became the third largest party in the House of Commons. Both UKIP and the Green Party increased their national share of the vote but failed to win any new seats (each of them ended up with one). The much-discussed new era of multiparty politics had failed to arrive—or at least, had failed to deliver the predicted close result.[3] It is possible that the multiparty debates of GE2015 will prove to be a one-off, an experiment which will never be repeated. In the meantime, though, they offer a unique set of data with which to explore this book's questions about gender, language, and politics.

THE CASE STUDY

The case study approach (Stake 1995; Yin 2009) is applied to complex phenomena which need to be understood in relation to their context of occurrence. It aims to enhance understanding of the phenomenon under study by concentrating on a single instance (or sometimes, a set of related instances), which is examined in detail from a number of different angles, using a range of data sources and often a mixture of analytic methods. Typically, this approach is used to study instances which are unique, in the sense that they are products of specific circumstances which cannot be exactly reproduced outside their original context. Case studies are not amenable to replication, and their primary goal is not to produce large-scale generalizations, but to understand the specific instance under study as fully as possible. However, one instance may be compared with others with which it shares relevant characteristics: often a case is selected for study because it exemplifies some more general phenomenon in which the researcher is interested.

The general phenomenon we are interested in is the political speech of women in public contexts where the prevailing linguistic norms are

---

[3] It would be a different story if the UK abandoned the first-past-the-post system, which rewards parties whose support is geographically concentrated rather than dispersed. The SNP was able to win fifty-six seats with a 4.7 % share of all votes cast nationally, whereas UKIP only won one seat with a 12.6 % share. More individuals cast votes for UKIP than for the Liberal Democrats, who won eight seats; there was a significant increase in UKIP's support, but it did not translate into an increase in Parliamentary representation because UKIP voters in almost all constituencies were outnumbered by supporters of some other party. (Figures sourced from the BBC News website, http://www.bbc.co.uk/news/election/2015/results, accessed 21 September 2015.)

adversarial. The specific instances we examine in detail are two televised party leaders' debates which were broadcast during the 2015 General Election campaign in the UK. The campaign as a whole formed the immediate context in relation to which these events must be understood; it will also be necessary to place them in a larger context, considering questions about, for instance, the nature of British party politics, the position of women in UK political institutions, the role played by the media in elections, and so on. The debates were selected for close study because of a feature that made them, in the context of British politics to date, unique: the presence of three women among the seven speakers who took part in them. These were cases in which an almost equal number of men and women spoke, from a position of notional equality (i.e. all had the status of party leaders), in the same events, under the same conditions. We examine these events from two main angles. In Chap. 2 our analysis focuses on *production*: the actual linguistic behaviour of participants in the two broadcast debates. The data analysed for this purpose are transcripts made from video recordings of the broadcasts. In Chap. 3 we examine the media *reception and representation* of the women participants and their speech, using data from a sample of election press coverage.

It might be asked whether a case study of three women's performances in two events during one political campaign is too narrow in scope to give much insight into the larger questions about language, gender, and politics which we have explored in this preliminary chapter. Our initial plan was to examine a variety of different political speech events and genres, involving a larger number of women who participated in GE2015 in various roles—not only as leaders of their parties, but also as senior office-holders in parties led by men; as designated party spokespeople on women's issues; or simply as 'ordinary' Parliamentary candidates. That approach would have had its virtues, but when we began to look in detail at the debates, we realized that the complexity and much of the interest of these data would be obscured by too selective and condensed a presentation. The debates needed to be analysed in some depth, and in a study of this length, we could only achieve depth by sacrificing breadth. We therefore chose to focus more specifically on the two debates, adopting a principle which is emphasized in many discussions of the case study approach: that the instance under study should be conceptualized as a 'multifaceted' object, whose multiple facets can be revealed by examining it from various angles and posing a range of different questions about it (these will be discussed more fully in the case study chapters themselves, but the questions we listed earlier in this chapter (p. 4, 16-17) give an indication of the range). Because they involve the in-depth investigation of something which is complex, multifaceted, and context dependent, case studies are typically carried out using a 'mixed method' approach. This one is no exception. The analytic tools we use do not reflect a theoretical commitment to one particular framework, but have been chosen for their usefulness in relation to our research questions. As we noted earlier, our approach is essentially qualitative: in the 'production' part of the case study (Chap. 2), we do make use of some basic frequency counting in order to identify large-scale patterns in, for instance, the distribution of turns and of speaking time among participants, but we are most interested in looking qualitatively at the linguistic and interactional behaviours which produce these quantitative patterns. In relation to the allocation of speaking time (an important resource for which participants in these debates competed), we will make use of some of the principles of Conversation Analysis (CA), and specifically on the model of turn-taking proposed by Sacks, Schegloff, and Jefferson (1974), which enables us to consider how participants took, held, and yielded the floor. To understand what they did with the floor, we will draw on insights from interactional sociolinguistics, an approach concerned with explicating the implicit meanings of interactional moves (Schiffrin 1994) and how these may be signalled by speakers to interlocutors and audiences (Gumperz 2001)—though we will also draw on our own and other researchers' understandings of the broader sociocultural and political context in which the interactions being analysed took place. In the part of the case study that deals with the media representation of the debates and the politicians who participated in them (Chap. 3), we use a mixture of qualitative content analysis, identifying major themes in the coverage we analyse, and discourse analysis in the 'critical' tradition (e.g. Fairclough 2010; van Dijk 1993), examining salient formal and rhetorical features of the language used in texts to show how certain understandings of the world—in this case, of gender, language, and politics—may be (re)circulated and naturalized through particular patterns of linguistic choice. Our overall approach to the questions we have posed will be informed throughout by insights drawn from a number of relevant research traditions, including work on broadcast talk (e.g. Scannell 1991; Montgomery 2001), language ideologies (e.g. Irvine 1989; Silverstein 1979), and, of course, language and gender, the main field of inquiry in which this book is located.

Clearly, more could be said about our data than we will be able to say in the space of this book. The questions we have set out in this chapter, about the status and workings of the 'different voice' ideology in contemporary political discourse, are not the only questions about language and gender that it would be possible, or interesting, to explore in an analysis of GE2015. However, those are the questions we have chosen to focus on. We begin in Chap. 2 by examining the debates themselves, and the linguistic behaviour of the politicians who took part in them.

REFERENCES

Baron-Cohen, S. (2003). *The essential difference: Men, women and the extreme male brain*. London: Allen Lane.

Baxter, J. (2010). *The language of female leadership*. London; New York, NY: Palgrave Macmillan.

Beard, M. (2014). The public voice of women. *London Review of Books, 36*(6), 11–14.

Beckett, C. (2015). The battle for the stage: Broadcasting. In P. Cowley & D. Kavanagh (Eds.), *The British General Election of 2015* (pp. 278–301). Basingstoke, Hampshire: Palgrave Macmillan.

Cameron, D. (1997). New labour, no feminism? *Trouble & Strife, 35*, 69–72.

Cameron, D. (2003). Gender and language ideologies. In J. Holmes & M. Meyerhoff (Eds.), *The handbook of language and gender* (pp. 447–467). Malden, MA: Blackwell.

Cameron, D. (2007). *The myth of Mars and Venus: Do men and women really speak different languages?* Oxford: Oxford University Press.

Chamorro-Premuzic, T. (2013). Why do so many incompetent men become leaders? *Harvard Business Review*, August 22 [online]. https://hbr.org/2013/08/why-do-so-many-incompetent-men.

Chaney, P. (2012). Critical actors vs. critical mass: The substantive representation of women in the Scottish Parliament. *British Journal of Politics and International Relations, 14*, 441–457.

Childs, S. (2004). A feminised style of politics? Women MPs in the House of Commons. *British Journal of Politics and International Relations, 6*(1), 3–19.

Childs, S., & Krook, M. L. (2009). Analyzing women's substantive representation: From critical mass to critical actors. *Government and Opposition, 44*(2), 125–145.

Eckert, P., & McConnell-Ginet, S. (1992). Communities of practice: Where language, gender and power all live. In K. Hall, M. Bucholtz, & B. Moonwomon (Eds.), *Locating power: Proceedings of the second Berkeley women and language conference* (pp. 89–99). Berkeley, CA: Berkeley Women and Language Group.

Fairclough, N. (2010). *Critical discourse analysis: The critical study of language* (2nd ed.). London: Longman.

Fox, R. L., & Lawless, J. L. (2011). Gendered perceptions and political candidacies: a central barrier to women's equality in electoral politics. *American Journal of Political Science, 55*(1), 59–73.

Gilligan, C. (1982). *In a different voice*. Harvard: Harvard University Press.

Goodwin, M. H. (2006). *The hidden life of girls: Games of stance, status and exclusion*. Malden, MA: Blackwell.

Grey, J. (1992). *Men are from Mars, Women are from Venus*. New York: HarperCollins.

Gumperz, J. (2001). Interactional sociolinguistics: A personal perspective. In D. Schiffrin, D. Tannen, & H. Hamilton (Eds.), *The handbook of discourse analysis* (pp. 213–228). Malden, MA: Wiley-Blackwell.

Holmes, J. (2006). *Gendered talk in the workplace*. Oxford: Blackwell.

Irvine, J. T. (1989). When talk isn't cheap: Language and political economy. *American Ethnologist, 16*, 248–267.

Karpowitz, C., & Mendelberg, T. (2014). *The silent sex*. Princeton: Princeton University Press.

Karpowitz, C., Mendelberg, T., & Shaker, L. (2012). Gender inequality in deliberative participation. *American Political Science Review, 106*(3), 533–547.

Kathlene, L. (1994). Power and influence in state legislative policymaking: The interaction of gender and position in committee hearing debates. *American Political Science Review, 88*(3), 560–576.

Krook, M. L., & Mackay, F. (Eds.). (2011). *Gender, politics and institutions: Towards a feminist institutionalism*. Basingstoke: Palgrave Macmillan.

Mackay, F. (2004). Gender and political representation in the UK: The state of the 'discipline'. *British Journal of Politics and International Relations, 6*(1), 99–100.

McDowell, J. (2015). Masculinity and non-traditional occupations: Men's talk in women's work, *Gender. Work & Organization, 22*(3), 273–291.

McElhinny, B. (1995). Challenging hegemonic masculinities: Female and male police officers handling domestic violence. In K. Hall & M. Buchholtz (Eds.), *Gender articulated: Language and the socially constructed self* (pp. 217–244). New York: Routledge.

Montgomery, M. (2001). The uses of authenticity: 'Speaking from experience' in a UK election broadcast. *The Communication Review, 4*(4), 447–462.

Phillips, S. U. (2003). The power of gender ideologies in discourse. In J. Holmes & M. Meyerhoff (Eds.), *The handbook of language and gender* (pp. 252–276). Malden, MA: Blackwell.

Rawnsley, A. (2006). Gordon Brown is from Mars, David Cameron is from Venus. *Observer*, 19 November.

Roberts, Y. (2015). Yet again men hold power: Why can't the Labour Party change? *Guardian*, 13 September [online]. http://www.theguardian.com/commentisfree/2015/sep/13/women-politics-power-labour-leadership-jeremy-corbyn? CMP=share_btn_tw.

Rudman, L. A. (1998). Self-promotion as a risk factor for women: The costs and benefits of counterstereotypical impression management. *Journal of Personality and Social Psychology, 74,* 629–645.

Rudman, L. A., & Fairchild, R. (2004). Reactions to counterstereotypic behaviour: The role of backlash in cultural stereotype maintenance. *Journal of Personality and Social Psychology, 87,* 157–176.

Scannell, P. (Ed.). (1991). *Broadcast talk.* London: Sage Publications.

Schiffrin, D. (1994). *Approaches to discourse.* Oxford: Blackwell.

Shaw, S. (2000). Language, gender and floor apportionment in political debates. *Discourse & Society, 11*(3), 401–418.

Shaw, S. (2006). Governed by the rules? The female voice in Parliamentary debates. In J. Baxter (Ed.), *Speaking out: The female voice in public contexts* (pp. 81–102). Basingstoke: Palgrave Macmillan.

Sherzer, J. (1987). A diversity of voices: Men's and women's speech in ethnographic perspective. In S. Phillips, S. Steele, & C. Tanz (Eds.), *Language, gender and sex in comparative perspective* (pp. 95–120). New York: Cambridge University Press.

Silverstein, M. (1979). Language structure and linguistic ideology. In P. Clyne, W. F. Hanks, & C. L. Hofbauer (Eds.), *The elements: A parasession on linguistic units and levels* (pp. 193–247). Chicago: Chicago Linguistic Society.

Stake, R. E. (1995). *The art of case-study research.* London: Sage.

Tannen, D. (1990). *You just don't understand: Men and women in conversation.* New York: Ballantine.

Tannen, D. (1994). *Gender and discourse.* New York: Oxford University Press.

Uchida, A. (1998). When 'difference' is 'dominance': A critique of the 'anti-power-based' cultural approach to sex differences. In D. Cameron (Ed.), *The feminist critique of language* (pp. 280–292). London: Routledge.

van Dijk, T. A. (1993). Principles of critical discourse analysis. *Discourse & Society, 4*(2), 249–283.

Walsh, C. (2001). *Gender and discourse: Language and power in politics, the church and institutions.* London: Longman.

Way, N. (2013). *Deep secrets: Boys' friendships and the crisis of connection.* Cambridge: Harvard University Press.

Yin, R. K. (2009). *Case study research, design and method* (4th ed.). London: Sage Publications.

CHAPTER 2

Gender and Speech Styles in the 2015 General Election Debates

Abstract This chapter presents an analysis of the linguistic behaviour of the party leaders who took part in the two televised debates that were central events in the GE2015 campaign. We consider the distribution of speaking turns and speaking time among participants, and examine the use they made of adversarial and cooperative/supportive strategies. The analysis shows that all participants employed a variety of strategies, though the range and balance was different for each individual. These individual differences were seen within as well as between gender groups: overall, gender appeared to be a less significant influence on leaders' performances than the relative status of their parties and the extent of their political and public speaking experience.

Keywords Adversarial discourse • Cooperation and competition • Debate • Interruption • Gendered speech styles • Turn-taking

INTRODUCTION

The participation of three women leaders in GE2015 offers an opportunity to examine the relationship between gender and political speech in the UK in a way that has not been possible before. In this chapter we ask: How did these women speak? Did their style of discourse differ from that

© The Editor(s) (if applicable) and The Author(s) 2016   27
D. Cameron, S. Shaw, *Gender, Power and Political Speech*,
DOI 10.1057/978-1-137-58752-7_2

of the men who participated in the same speech events? We also consider the similarities and differences among the women themselves.

Following the dissolution of Parliament on 30 March, the party leaders participated in a range of campaign events, including regional and national party rallies; visits to workplaces, schools, and hospitals; and multiple interviews, discussions, and debates broadcast on radio and television. Undoubtedly, they deployed different styles of communication across these different contexts. Here, though, we will focus on their performances in the two televised national debates which were arguably the most important public speech events of GE2015: the ITV 'Leaders' debate' which took place on 2 April 2015 and the BBC 'Challengers' debate' held on 16 April 2015. The debates are of particular interest for two reasons: first, because they belong to an inherently adversarial speech genre, of the type which is often said to pose problems for women, and second, because they permit direct comparisons between male and female speakers. The debates were the only occasions during the campaign where the party leaders participated in the same speech event under the same conditions, and where they were able to interact directly with one another.

TELEVISED POLITICAL DEBATES

Televised debates, although firmly established in other contexts (e.g. US presidential and gubernatorial elections), are relatively new in the UK. The first televised leaders' debates in 2010, between the then-Prime Minister Gordon Brown and the leaders of the main opposition parties, David Cameron and Nick Clegg, were said to have formed the 'spine' of the election campaign (Kavanagh and Cowley 2010: 147), with the three debates attracting a total audience of twenty-two million people. Although the two 2015 debates fell short of that figure (with approximately sixteen million viewers), they can still be seen as 'a significant part of the UK election campaign's claim to democratic authority' (Beckett 2015). They were also key events in the reporting of the campaign across the British media: the extensive commentary they generated is likely to have contributed to the way the party leaders were perceived by anyone who consumed any kind of media election coverage, whether or not they had watched the debates themselves.

Debates in general can be formally described as 'the most extreme transformation of conversation – most extreme in fully fixing the most important (and perhaps nearly all) of the parameters that conversation allows to vary'

(Sacks et al. 1974: 731). One obvious example is the allocation of the floor, which in everyday conversation is jointly accomplished by the participants. In debates, by contrast, turn-taking is regulated to ensure, ideally, that all speakers participate equally. In practice, this ideal is rarely upheld: the rules are frequently transgressed, and the actual progress of debates falls well short of the equitable distribution of speaking rights (Adams 1992, 2015; Christie 2003; Edelsky and Adams 1990; Ilie 2013; Shaw 2000; 2006; forthcoming). Televised debates vary in how strictly contributions are timed or otherwise regulated, how much spontaneous interaction is permitted, and how much control participants can exert over the topics discussed. Some speeches can be prepared in advance (particularly the pre-allocated speaking turns that conventionally open and close a debate), and it is assumed that speakers will rehearse elements of their delivery before the event. However, analysts of broadcast discourse have noted the value accorded to 'authentic talk', in which 'traces of scriptedness or rehearsal for performance are avoided, effaced or suppressed' (Montgomery 2001a: 460).

The layout or 'staging' of a televised event can also affect the style of interaction. 'Wisecracks' and backchannels have been found to be more common when participants were seated close together in a 'talk-show' set design. At the other extreme, sets where the participants had to walk up to a microphone to take their speaking turns 'severely limited all kinds of uninvited speakings' (Edelsky and Adams 1990: 181). Other characteristics of the TV debate genre are dependent on editorial and production decisions linked to the broadcasting process, such as the selection of tight or wide camera angles and cut-away shots. These production processes also extend to directions given to the moderator via 'in-ear monitors' from the director's gallery in relation to the timing and sequence of the allocation of debate turns and topics. This means that there is a blurring of the distinction between the frontstage performance of the debate and the backstage pre-planning, rehearsal, and direction.

In order to be successful in TV debates, political leaders must manage a range of often opposing demands. They must construct themselves as an authentic, credible, and popular 'public figure' (Corner 2000), appearing confident but not self-satisfied, passionate but not zealous, and confrontational but not aggressive. They must exude the gravitas that their position demands without appearing cold or detached. In this deliberate dispute genre, they are expected to argue their case convincingly and expose the weaknesses of others. Even more than political discourse in general, political dispute genres have often been associated with 'masculine' speech styles (Lovenduski 2014). Direct competition and argument are considered to be at odds with women's communication styles, which are supposedly characterized by collaboration, cooperation, and consensus building. Televised political debates are therefore particularly pertinent events in which to examine the relationship between gender and political speech.

That relationship has been examined by researchers working in contexts where the televised debate is a well-established genre. Early work in the USA by Edelsky and Adams (1990) and Adams (1992) focused on six debates involving candidates for gubernatorial and state representative positions. They found that disorderly behaviour was common: powerful speakers violated the ideal, equitable progression of turns by interrupting (which affects the length of other speakers' turns), and selecting and maintaining the topic of a turn. The researchers defined 'out of order' or 'non-debate-like' talk to include different types of 'uninvited turns' or UNs, and their functions or 'moves' were placed in categories such as 'wisecracks', 'complaints', and 'demeaning' UNs. Overall, their research suggested there was most equality in the number and length of turns when the debate format was closest to the canonical ideal in which turns were invited by the moderator and there was little or no possibility of UNs. Gender differences were greatest when there was most 'slippage' between the ideal and the actual progression of the debate. As Edelsky and Adams comment (1990: 186):

> Even though these participants entered respective events with other differently allocated resources (e.g. experience, political affiliation and incumbency), they also produced variable power over resources in the debate itself. Men got better treatment (safer turn spaces, extra turns, follow ups on their topics) and they took control of more resources (more time for their positions, more of the 'aggressive' speakings).

These findings underline the critical role of the moderator in determining the distribution of speaking turns, but they also suggest that men are typically more powerful in debates than women, taking longer turns and making more aggressive moves. However, Edelsky and Adams found some variability in the women's behaviour: one of the female candidates in the study was 'more willing to disrupt the rules'. She was the only woman to make a 'demeaning' move and enter into 'friendly repartee with moderators' (Edelsky and Adams 1990: 185). The explanation the researchers suggest is that this candidate was a 'Party insider' debating with two male party outsiders: 'insider status may have overridden gender in this case'.

In some contexts gender may itself be linked to insider/outsider status. In research on the related genre of Parliamentary debates in the UK
House of Commons, Shaw (2000; forthcoming) found that women MPs
in two data samples, one from 1998 to 2001 and one from 2009 to 2011,
very rarely made illegal challenges such as interrupting a speaker from a
sitting position. Basing her argument on an ethnographic description of
the Westminster Parliament's established norms and practices, Shaw suggests that the women MPs' status as outsiders (they are a minority in an
institution which excluded them for centuries) positions them as 'interlopers' (Eckert 1998), and that this leads them to pay meticulous attention to
the rules, as a way of proving their 'worthiness' to belong.

In the House of Commons, speaking out of turn can be analysed as a
form of gendered (male) behaviour. But this cannot be treated as an invari-
ant pattern: as Baxter (2010: 168) observes, 'each context may have subtly
varying expectations and requirements of a person's gendered identity'.
In the devolved legislative assemblies of Scotland, Wales, and Northern
Ireland, Shaw (forthcoming) did not observe the same gendered pattern
of rule-breaking she had found in the House of Commons. In these newer
institutions, which aspired to gender-egalitarian ideals from the outset
and included women as founder members, women broke the interactional
rules as frequently as their male colleagues. Women resisted the moderator,
spoke out of turn, and—particularly in the Scottish Parliament—engaged
in out-of-order 'banter' on the debate floor. This finding is potentially
relevant to the analysis of the GE2015 leaders' debates, since two of the
women leaders, Leanne Wood and Nicola Sturgeon, are members of
devolved assemblies; their experience in these more egalitarian settings
may have a bearing on their behaviour in other contexts.

It should also be acknowledged that more recent studies of US televised
debates have not found the gender differences noted in early work. A study
by Adams (2015) found that in US gubernatorial debates, women candidates' linguistic strategies were varied, noting that one candidate did not
downgrade her opponents but had 'expert control over the turn-taking
structure', which reinforced an authoritative style of coordination and competition. In contrast, a different woman candidate 'downgraded' frequently
and 'limited joint activity by talking over her male opponents and ignoring
their responses' (Adams 2015: 244). Another analysis of two gubernatorial
and two Senate debates (Banwart and McKinney 2005) coded the politicians' contributions for a range of characteristics, including those thought to
represent stereotypically masculine and feminine verbal styles. They found
no significant differences between men and women in relation to their use

of features such as negative attacks on opponents, different types of appeals (e.g. logical or emotional), what issues they emphasized (e.g. taxes, the economy, education), and which character traits they alluded to (e.g. past performance, experience in politics, commonality with constituents). They concluded that there were more similarities than differences in the debating styles of men and women and that both displayed what they label 'gendered adaptiveness' (Banwart and McKinney 2005: 370):

> Although masculine character traits (e.g. aggressiveness) are much more frequently emphasized by both female and male candidates than are feminine character traits, both female and male candidates develop their debate responses by using feminine communication strategies (e.g. personal use of tone) more frequently than masculine character strategies.

This study suggests it is problematic to assume that the dominant speech style in televised political debates is stereotypically 'masculine'. Rather, the genre seems to call for a 'mixed' style, combining personalization and direct address to the audience with more conventional 'cut-and-thrust' forms of argument. Many analysts have pointed out that 'authenticity' and 'sincerity' are important values in broadcasting, especially on television (Montgomery 2001a, 2010): this encourages the 'feminine' strategies of personalization and direct address, contributing to what Fairclough (1992: 204) has called 'the conversationalization of public discourse'. Transferring linguistic strategies associated with the private sphere to public speech events projects 'a cluster of values widely held to be desirable: egalitarianism; informality, intimacy, greater possibilities for participation and so on' (Montgomery 2001b: 298).

In the light of this discussion, our analysis of the GE2015 debates will focus on two broad issues: first, the management of the floor and the distribution of speaking turns; and second, the linguistic strategies participants used to position themselves and their opponents. These two things are not, of course, completely separable (some floor management strategies, like interrupting, may serve the dual purpose of gaining a speaking turn and constructing the interrupter as assertive, authoritative, or passionate; some rhetorical strategies, like asking an opponent a question that implies a flaw in their argument, may also have the effect of ceding the floor to them). The structure of the following sections acknowledges this, moving from an initial focus on the overall mechanics of floor management and distribution of turns among participants to a more fine-grained analysis of particular

Debate structure	Duration (minutes)
1. Opening Statements – each speaker allocated one-minute secure turn	7
2a) Question one – Question from the audience ('Johnny') on spending cuts each speaker allocated one minute 'secure' response	7
2b) 'Free flowing' debate on the question regulated by moderator	16
3a) Question two – Question from the audience ('Terry') on the NHS each speaker allocated one minute 'secure' response	7
3b)'Free flowing' debate on the question regulated by the moderator	15
4a) Question three – Question from the audience ('Joan') on immigration each speaker allocated one minute 'secure' response	7
4b) 'Free flowing' debate on the question regulated by the moderator	16
5a) Question four – Question from the audience ('Rebecca') on the financial future for younger people.	7
5b) 'Free flowing' debate on the question regulated by the moderator	15
6. Closing statements - each speaker allocated one-minute secure turn	7

Fig. 2.1 The structure of the ITV debate

sequences, in which we consider not only how the floor was gained, held, or ceded, but also what participants used their turns to do and what strategies they employed in doing it. The final section returns to the central issue of gender and political speech, drawing on the totality of the analysis presented.

The data analysed were transcribed from video recordings of the two debates (the ITV debate lasting two hours and the BBC debate ninety minutes).[1] Initially, we transcribed each debate in full using a 'broad' transcription scheme that allowed us to count individual leaders' speaking turns and measure the time they spent speaking in each debate (see the next section). Having established the overall structure of the debates (see Fig. 2.1), we then transcribed specific extracts in more detail for finer-grained analysis of speakers' turn-taking strategies (Sacks et al. 1974), and their use of certain 'contextualization cues' (Gumperz 2001: 221). Non-verbal communication was not routinely transcribed since the details of speakers' facial expressions, gaze direction, gestures, and so on were not consistently visible in the broadcasts we were working from.[2] We will

---

[1] Broadcasts were made available online at http://www.bbc.co.uk/iplayer/episode/b05r0s83/the-itv-leaders-debate, http://www.bbc.co.uk/iplayer/episode/b05r87pr/bbc-election-debate-2015, and via Box of Broadcasts, http://bobnational.net/site/index.

[2] The participants in each debate stood behind podiums arranged in a shallow horseshoe formation so that, on screen, they appeared in a row: their positions from right to left were decided by drawing lots.

sometimes comment on these details where they are both clearly visible and pertinent to the analysis, but we will not discuss them in general terms.

MANAGING THE DEBATE FLOOR

We begin with the basic question of how speaking turns and talking time were distributed in the first debate, in which seven party leaders participated. For the purposes of analysis, a turn is defined as every verbal contribution made by a speaker regardless of its length or its success in gaining the floor. We adopted this definition because our initial aim was to record all attempts made by each speaker to intervene in the debate, including those which did not get beyond a single word or which were produced simultaneously with another participant's contribution. Later on in the analysis, we distinguish between different types of turns (e.g. invited and uninvited), and reproduce longer transcribed sequences. Our initial analysis does however consider how much time each participant spent speaking: this was measured by noting the time code from the video recording on the transcript for each turn to the nearest second.

The rules described above, combined with the structure shown in Fig. 2.1, produced an unequal distribution of both turns and speaking time among the seven participants in the ITV debate, as shown in Fig. 2.2.

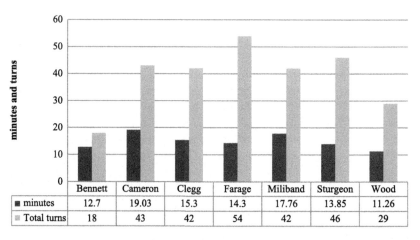

	Bennett	Cameron	Clegg	Farage	Miliband	Sturgeon	Wood
■ minutes	12.7	19.03	15.3	14.3	17.76	13.85	11.26
▨ Total turns	18	43	42	54	42	46	29

Fig. 2.2 Turns and speaking time taken by each politician in the ITV debate

At first glance there appears to be a gendered pattern here: all the male participants speak for more time, measured in minutes, than any of the female ones. However, the number of speaking turns taken by participants does not show the same pattern: Farage and Sturgeon took the largest number, followed by Cameron, then Clegg and Miliband, with Wood and Bennett (especially the latter) some way behind. The two speakers who took most turns were not the same two who took most speaking time. To understand this, it is necessary to look more closely at how the floor was managed. It is not simply that some speakers were more active than others in competing for the floor, but also that some had more opportunities than others to contribute.

There were three main ways in which turns were allocated during free-flowing segments. Participants could be invited to speak by the moderator, they could be nominated by another participant who addressed or referred to them directly (this is akin to the conversational mechanism glossed by Sacks et al. (1974) as 'current speaker selects next'), or they could self-select and take an uninvited turn (UN). The moderator's use of the first mechanism was evidently influenced by others' use of the second: direct references to one participant by another often prompted the moderator to allocate the next turn to the participant who had been referred to. Figure 2.3

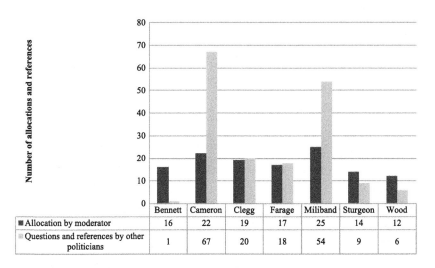

Fig. 2.3 Moderator-allocated turns and references by other politicians in the ITV debate

shows the number of moderator-allocated turns and references by others for each of the debate participants:

One thing this figure shows is that the moderator in the first debate, Julie Etchingham, allocated more turns to the male than to the female leaders. It also shows that the two men who get most directly allocated turns, Miliband and Cameron, are also those who are referred to most frequently by other participants (on that measure, they are significantly ahead of all the others). How these turn allocation mechanisms work and what their combined effect is can be illustrated using an extract from the first free-flowing segment (2b in Fig. 2.1). The leader selected to open this part of the proceedings was Nick Clegg, and the extract begins with the moderator's invitation to him to speak (Fig. 2.4 and Extract 1):

Transcription symbols

{   start of overlapping utterance with the line above/below

}   end of overlapping utterance with the line above/below

under<u>line</u>   particular emphasis on word or syllable

(.)   micro-pause of under a second

(1)   timed pause in seconds

CAPS   high volume (shouting)

(unclear)   indecipherable

=   latching (no pause)
(Based on Jefferson 2004)

Participants
NB = Natalie Bennett; DC = David Cameron; NC = Nick Clegg; NF = Nigel Farage; DM = David Miliband; NS = Nicola Sturgeon; LW = Leanne Wood; Aud = audience; JE = Julie Etchingham; DD = David Dimbleby

Fig. 2.4   Transcription 'key'

Extract 1

1 JE: Nick Clegg perhaps you could start the debate for us tonight (.)

2 NC: well I actually have a question f f for D D David Cameron because he's just said to

3   all of us that he wants to <u>stay</u> (.) the course (.) well that's not of course what the

4   Conservative party want to do at <u>all</u> (.) re<u>mar</u>kably the Conservative party have

5   said they are not going to ask the <u>ric</u>hest in society (.) to make a <u>single</u> extra

6   penny of contribution to balancing the books through the <u>tax</u> system (.) they

7   want to impose ideo<u>log</u>ically driven cuts on sch<u>ools</u> so that hat I hah I just I

8   when I hear the Conservatives talk about a choice between competence and

9   chaos (.) just i<u>mage</u> David Cameron the <u>chaos</u> in people's <u>lives</u> (.) the people who

10   in the NHS don't know whether you're going to find the <u>money</u> (.) the people who

11   don't know whether the <u>nur</u>sery or the <u>coll</u>ege or their sch<u>ools</u> are going to close

12   (.) <u>that</u>'s why Johnny's right (.) you need to take a <u>balanced</u> approach (.) you <u>do</u>

13   need to reduce spending but you also need to ask the richest (.) to make a

14   contribution it is the only <u>fair</u> way of finishing the ⌠<u>job</u>

15 JE: ⎱thank you⌠David Cameron⌉

16 DC: ⎱w well Nick⌡

17 DC: is <u>wrong</u> about our plans because of course we are going to raise five <u>bill</u>ion from

18   tax evasion and aggressive tax avoidance as we've done (.) in this <u>par</u>liament and

19   that's <u>par</u>t of the balanced plan that also involves (.) putting more money into

20   our NHS and cutting taxes (.)

21   ⌠for working people but <u>here</u>'s the point (.)   ⌉

22 NC: ⎱you're not going to ask the very wealthy to pay an extra penny⌡

23 DC: but here (.)⌠well the very wealthy include some⌉ of the tax avoiders and

24 JE: ⎱ thank you let David Cameron finish⌡

25 DC: evaders but here's the point (.) we've got to understand why the deficit matters

26   and why we <u>got</u> here and the problem and the real <u>choice</u> is with Ed Miliband

27   who <u>still</u> thinks the last Labour government didn't tax too much borrow too

28   much and <u>spend</u> too much (.) and if you <u>don</u>'t understand the mistakes of the

29   past (.) you <u>can</u>'t provide the leadership for the <u>future</u>=

30 JE: =Ed Miliband

This extract shows Clegg opening the segment with an attacking question directed at David Cameron (lines 2–14), which prompts the moderator to invite Cameron to respond. Clegg interrupts Cameron (line 22), and this is censured by the moderator, securing Cameron's speaking turn (line 24). Cameron then shifts his attack to Miliband and the moderator responds by inviting Miliband to reply (line 30). The floor is regulated through a combination of turns that are pre-allocated by the moderator, turns that are 'uninvited' but that respond to an accusation, and turns that are allocated by the moderator as a result of a reference (or question or accusation) directed at one politician by another. The more a politician is addressed or mentioned in this way, the more speaking turns she/he accrues. In practice, this favours the politicians who represent the largest parties and hold the most significant offices (Cameron and Clegg as incumbent leaders of the coalition government, and Miliband as leader of the main opposition party). Sturgeon, Wood, Farage, and Bennett lead less significant parties, and are therefore referred to less, which means they get a smaller share of the allocated speaking time. The most important factor producing differences in participants' access to the floor, therefore, is not gender as such but a participant's political role and the status of the party she/he represents.

As mentioned above, though, there is another way in which politicians are able to accrue speaking turns: they can take the floor uninvited. Figure 2.5 shows the number of invited and uninvited turns taken by each participant in the debate, and Fig. 2.6 shows what percentage of each speaker's turns were invited or uninvited. (Uninvited turns (UNs) are defined as any turn not invited by the moderator.)

It is Farage and Sturgeon who take the most UNs, and UNs represent a strikingly high proportion of their turns. Since all participants are equally in a position to intervene uninvited, this is a means by which they can attempt to compensate for being allocated fewer invited turns than the main party leaders. But the compensation is only partial, because the two types of turns are not equal. Invited turns are more secure: they are legitimated by the moderator, who may police attempts to encroach on them, so they generally permit the speaker to make at least one point in full. With UNs, by contrast, the floor has to be won, and the speaker's occupation of it is always liable to be censured by the moderator or contested by other participants. In terms of speaking time, it is the politicians with high proportions of *invited* turns who have the advantage, and this is reflected in Fig. 2.2. Farage's pattern of participation demonstrates

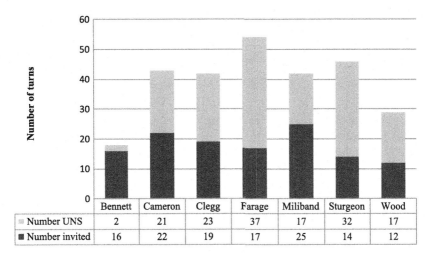

	Bennett	Cameron	Clegg	Farage	Miliband	Sturgeon	Wood
Number UNS	2	21	23	37	17	32	17
Number invited	16	22	19	17	25	14	12

Fig. 2.5 The number of invited and uninvited turns (UNs) and total number of turns taken by politicians in the ITV debate

	Bennett	Cameron	Clegg	Farage	Miliband	Sturgeon	Wood
percent uninvited turns	11	48	55	68	40	69	59
percent invited turns	89	52	45	32	60	31	41

Fig. 2.6 Percentage of invited and uninvited turns taken by each politician in the ITV debate

the point: although he takes more turns than anyone else, only 32 % of these are invited, and he occupies the floor for less time than Cameron, Clegg, and Miliband, whose contributions include a much higher percentage of invited turns. As representatives of the most important parties, they are given more secure opportunities to speak.

Because gender is closely linked to party status—the leaders of the main parties are all men, while the women party leaders all represent less significant parties—it is not possible to identify a pattern of participation related to gender alone. It should be noted, however, that there is variation among the three women. Bennett only takes two UNs, but Sturgeon and Wood take over half of their turns uninvited. These percentages indicate that women can and do make unsanctioned interventions to gain additional speaking turns.

	Bennett	Cameron	Clegg	Farage	Miliband	Sturgeon	Wood
Interruptions	1	16	17	25	17	27	11
Total UNs	2	21	23	37	17	32	17

Fig. 2.7   Interruptions and UNs in the ITV debate

In this connection it is interesting to examine the (large) subset of UNs which are interruptions—that is, interventions which occur when another speaker's turn is clearly still ongoing.[3] 'Folk' versions of the 'different voice' ideology (like those quoted in the introduction to Chap. 1) often mention women politicians' greater reluctance to interrupt or talk over other speakers as one of the things that makes their style different from men's. Analysis of this first debate, however, does not entirely support that perception. Figure 2.7 shows how frequently each of the seven participants interrupted another speaker, set alongside the total number of UNs taken by each of them.

This figure reveals that the two participants who had the highest overall frequency of UNs and the highest number of interruptions were a man and a woman, Farage and Sturgeon, respectively; he took more UNs overall, but she interrupted more frequently. Wood and Bennett, by contrast, were the participants whose frequency of interruption was lowest (there was also a significant gap between the two of them). Once again, gender appears to be less relevant here than party status—along with, perhaps especially in Bennett's case, individual experience and confidence. The most 'extreme' exploiters of interruption (and other kinds of uninvited interventions) were the two leaders of what might be called 'middle'-status parties. On the one hand, Farage and Sturgeon had more need to assert themselves via UNs than Cameron, Clegg, and Miliband since they were allocated fewer secure turns. On the other, their affiliation to the most significant of the smaller parties may have given them a greater sense than Wood and Bennett of their entitlement to speak without invitation.

It should be acknowledged that interruptions have a range of functions in interaction, not all of which are at odds with the description of women's speech style as cooperative and supportive. As Tannen (1993) has argued, interrupting or 'talking along with' another speaker in order to express

---

[3] We counted interruptions as occurring where there was no evidence for a 'Transition Relevance Place' (Sacks et al. 1974). The remaining UNs occurred at a Transition Relevance Place.

	Bennett	Cameron	Clegg	Farage	Miliband	Sturgeon	Wood	total
Agreement	1	2	3	4	0	0	1	11
Requests to moderator	0	1	1	0	7	1	0	10
Challenge or question	0	10	12	17	9	25	10	83
Respond to challenge or question	0	3	1	4	1	1	0	10

Fig. 2.8   Function of interruptions in the ITV debate

agreement or encouragement may function as a marker of 'high involvement', signalling enthusiasm for the speaker's contribution rather than a desire to cut it short and take over the floor. In this debate, there were some interruptions of that type, and others which took the form of appeals to the moderator to allocate the next turn to the interrupter. This is not a supportive move, but nor is it a direct challenge to the current speaker. However, debates are fundamentally adversarial speech events, and it is not surprising to find that the majority of interruptions did take the form of challenges (or questions that implied a challenge). Figure 2.8 shows the functions of interruptions in the ITV debate and how these were distributed among the seven participants.

With the exception of Bennett, all participants produced more interruptions in the 'challenge' category than in any other; but once again, it was Sturgeon who produced the highest number. She and Miliband also stand out for not having produced any of the most supportive types of interruptions.

The patterns we have identified in this analysis of the ITV debate recurred in the second, BBC debate (which featured only the 'challengers', while excluding the incumbent government leaders Cameron and Clegg). This debate, moderated by David Dimbleby, had a similar format to the first one. It retained the structure of opening statements, followed by five questions from members of the audience, a 'secure' one-minute response, and then 'free-flowing' moderated debate for each question, concluding with one-minute statements from each of the five participants. Figure 2.9 shows how turns and speaking time were distributed.

In this debate, with the incumbents absent, Miliband was the dominant participant, followed by Farage and Sturgeon, with Wood and Bennett significantly behind. As with the ITV debate, the number of turns taken did not map perfectly onto the speaking time measure. Farage took more turns than Sturgeon, but on this occasion, she spoke for longer.

Figure 2.10 shows the number of references to each participant and the turns allocated to each by the moderator. (The absent incumbents,

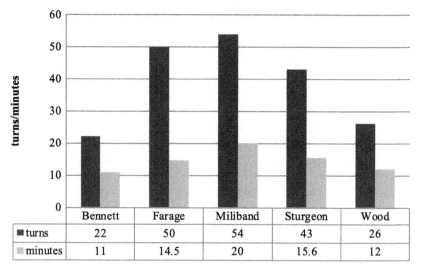

Fig. 2.9 Distribution of turns and speaking time in the BBC debate

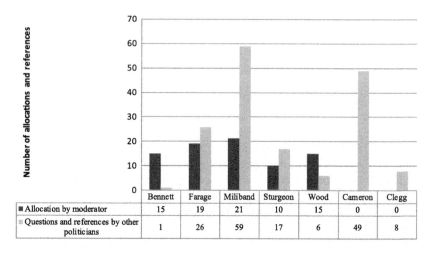

Fig. 2.10 Moderator-allocated turns and references by other politicians in the BBC debate

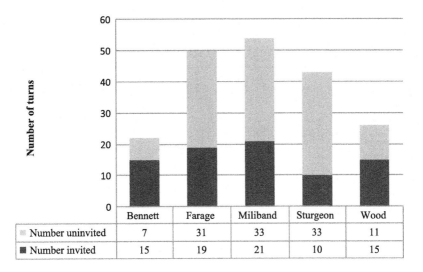

	Bennett	Farage	Miliband	Sturgeon	Wood
Number uninvited	7	31	33	33	11
Number invited	15	19	21	10	15

Fig. 2.11 Invited and uninvited turns in the BBC debate.

	Bennet	Farage	Miliband	Sturgeon	Wood
Percent invited	69	38	39	23	42
Percent uninvited	31	62	61	77	58

Fig. 2.12 Percentage of invited and uninvited turns taken by each politician in the BBC debate

Cameron and Clegg, were referred to frequently by other participants, and this is included in the data.)

Sturgeon manages to take forty-three turns despite having the smallest number actually allocated to her. It may be that the moderator allocates her fewer invited turns because her uninvited interventions are so successful. Figure 2.11 shows the number of invited and uninvited turns taken by each politician, and Fig. 2.12 the percentage of invited and uninvited turns.

Figure 2.13 shows the frequency of interruptions for the five participants in the BBC debate, and Fig. 2.14 shows their functions.

	Bennett	Farage	Miliband	Sturgeon	Wood
Interruptions	7	18	19	30	4
Total UNs	7	31	33	33	11

Fig. 2.13   Interruptions and UNs in the BBC debate

	Bennett	Farage	Miliband	Sturgeon	Wood	total
Agreement	2	3	0	0	1	6
Requests to moderator	0	0	5	2	0	7
Challenge or question	5	11	8	27	3	54
Respond to challenge or question	0	4	6	1	0	11

Fig. 2.14   Function of interruptions in the BBC debate

Again, Sturgeon was the most frequent interrupter; her main target was Miliband, who was the recipient of twenty-two of her thirty interruptions, and the main purpose for which she interrupted opponents (including Farage as well as Miliband) was to challenge or question them.

So far, we have shown that in the GE2015 televised debates, the floor was not equally distributed: some participants were advantaged relative to others by the number of invited turns they were allocated (over and above those which were pre-allocated to all leaders equally), and this reflected the extent to which they were mentioned or addressed by other participants (which in turn was closely linked to their and their party's status). However, we have also noted that participants were also able to claim the floor through UNs, and that this option was used most frequently by participants who did not enjoy an advantage in relation to invited turns—the leaders of smaller parties, particularly Farage and Sturgeon. A range of different kinds of interactional moves falls into the UN category, and those which are technically interruptions may serve a variety of purposes: in these data, the commonest was challenging or questioning an opponent. However, some interruptions and other UNs were more successful than others in terms of the additional speaking time that was gained through them, how far they set an agenda for subsequent discourse, and what benefit they produced for the speaker overall. It is therefore of interest to take a qualitative, more micro-analytic approach to the characteristics of UNs, and to examine the way they were used by different speakers during one of the 'free-flowing' segments of the BBC debate.

'Free-flowing' Debate: Gaining and Using the Floor

The first question from the audience in the BBC debate was asked by Charlotte Dennis, and its subject was government spending:

> As someone about to enter the job market, do you think it is fair to increase government spending like so many of you plan to do, when my generation will be left to pay off the debt?

This question related to the core political issue of the election, the Conservative–Liberal Democrat coalition government's policy, maintained since the previous general election in 2010, of reducing the government's financial deficit through cost-cutting or 'austerity' measures. The five politicians in the debate had already made their positions clear in their election manifestos, in the previous ITV debate and throughout the campaign. Broadly speaking, Ed Miliband and Nigel Farage were in favour of spending cuts, while Natalie Bennett, Nicola Sturgeon, and Leanne Wood opposed them. The question itself implied a 'pro-austerity' position, being mainly directed at the politicians who argued for stopping the cuts and increasing government spending.

Participants' 'secure' one-minute responses to this question reflected their already established positions. Nicola Sturgeon, who spoke first, said it was important to get the deficit down, but that she wanted to achieve this through 'modest increases to government spending' in order to 'get our economy growing'. Miliband spoke next, agreeing with the questioner and stating that his plan was to 'cut the deficit every year and balance the books', but instead of making cuts to public services, he would 'reverse David Cameron's tax cut for millionaires' and 'clamp down on tax avoidance'. The third speaker, Natalie Bennett, also agreed that reducing debt was important, but wanted to achieve it by investing money in social housing and renewable energy, and cutting university tuition fees to reduce personal debt. Nigel Farage started his secure turn by criticizing 'these guys' (Cameron and Clegg) for not reducing the deficit enough over the term of the previous government. He set himself apart from 'the people here tonight and the other two who went somewhere else this evening' by claiming that they 'are going to drive us into even greater debt'. He proposed a programme which would involve 'cutting our foreign aid budget, cutting our EU contributions, stopping white elephant projects like HS2 [a reference to a planned new high-speed rail link] and recalculating the Barnett Formula so less money goes over Hadrian's wall to Scotland'. Finally, Leanne Wood responded that 'Plaid Cymru does want to tackle the deficit but not at any cost' and that 'continuing on the path of austerity will deliver a very uncertain future for the next generations', whereas 'investing in job creation and public services now will offer them a much better future'. These positions provided the context for the subsequent 'free-flowing' debate.

The first turn was allocated by the moderator to Ed Miliband in a way that highlighted the opposition between him and Farage:

> Ed Miliband, Nigel Farage says he is the only one out of the five of you who plans to get out of a 1.5 trillion pound debt and forty-six billion pounds a year interest payments. Is he right?

Miliband responded with an unmitigated rejection of Farage's argument, saying 'No and his sums don't add up.' He claimed that Farage would 'follow David Cameron's plans to double the cuts next year' and 'cut the top rate of income tax even further for the highest earners'. Then, the moderator allocated Nigel Farage a turn, also referencing the opposition between him and Miliband with the question 'your sums don't add up?' Farage defended his economic policies, and the end of his turn marked the point where participants were free to compete for the floor by taking UNs. The beginning of this sequence is reproduced next:

Extract 2

1   NF: (end of Farage's turn) we have a real <u>prob</u>lem here and I haven't heard from <u>you</u>

2   (.) Ed (.) a <u>single</u> cut that you would make not <u>one</u> (.)

3   EM: now that's that's <u>wrong</u> Nigel=

4   NF: =well <u>tell</u> me=

5   EM: =well ⌈I'll tell you ⌉

6   NF: ⌊tell me (.) tell⌋me⌈how you're going⌉to balance the⌈books ⌉

7   EM: ⌊we've said that ⌋ ⌊we've said⌋that

8   for pensioners with incomes over forty-two thousand

9   pounds⌈(.) we⌉'ll take away the winter fuel allowance (.) that's a

10 NF   ⌊yeah ⌋

11 EM: difficult decision (.)

12 NF: yup

13 EM: we've shown how we can save <u>hun</u>dreds of millions of pounds

14   in local government in policing and⌈elsewhere⌉

15 NF: ⌊yup ⌋

----

16 EM: but I just want to⌈take issue I just⌈want to take issue I⌉just want to take issue⌉

17 NF: ⌊but that's all ⌊peanuts ⌋

18 DD: ⌊hold on hold on a second let me let me ⌋

----

19 EM: ⌈with this point (.) I want to take⌉ issue let me just take issue David about these

20 DD: ⌊bring one or two of the others in⌋

21   EM: spending cuts (.) ⌈because⌉ I really want the audience to understand

22   DD: ⌊alright ⌋

23   EM: this because Nigel hasn't denied that he wants to <u>double</u> the spending cuts next

24   year now he's got these <u>fan</u>tasy figures that somehow getting out of Europe is

25   going to save all of this money (.) when it is a di<u>saster</u> for jobs in our country (.)

26   the re<u>ality</u> is that for the NHS and education Nigel your plans are <u>dangerous</u> (.)

27   DD: ⌈alright   ⌉

28   EM: ⌊they are⌋ like David Cameron's plans and they are <u>dangerous</u> for our core public

29   services which Charlotte and many others rely on

This extract starts with Farage directly challenging Miliband on Labour's plans for spending cuts. Miliband responds directly with an UN (line 3), saying that Farage 'is wrong'. Farage then asks Miliband to tell him where Labour's spending cuts are going to fall, interrupting Miliband as he starts to answer (line 6). As Miliband continues to explain where the cuts will fall, Farage punctuates his answer with a series of minimal responses ('yeah' and 'yup', lines 10, 12, and 15) which function to put pressure on Miliband and also to contest the complete transference of the floor to another speaker. When Miliband attempts to change the topic (line 16), Farage criticizes Miliband's response to his original challenge using informal lexis, saying 'but that's all peanuts' (line 17). The moderator also picks up on this topic change and attempts to bring in other speakers who are gesturing that they want to intervene. Miliband appeals directly to the moderator to extend his turn and this is granted. Miliband continues to criticize Farage and finishes his point despite the moderator's attempt to bring his turn to an end with a regulatory 'alright' (line 22). Despite taking a number of (brief, overlapping) UNs, Farage does not succeed in reclaiming the floor during this sequence, whereas Miliband's appeal to the moderator for permission to finish his answer gains him an additional sanctioned turn. Miliband has the last word, and appears to 'win' this spontaneous exchange because he effectively launches an adversarial attack on Farage in a speaking turn that was originally allocated to Farage. If this is characteristic of Farage's interventions overall, that may explain why his relatively large number of turns does not translate into a larger share of speaking time. Similarly, if Miliband's behaviour in this extract is typical, it may explain how he is able to speak for the longest amount of time: he both accrues sanctioned speaking turns and takes UNs of substantial length.

Immediately after this, the moderator allocates a turn to Nicola Sturgeon:

Extract 3

1	DD:	alright Nicola Sturgeon do you agree with what Ed Miliband
2		⎧is saying⎫
3	NS:	⎩well (.) I⎭ I want to get rid of the Tories on May the seventh and I think that it's
4		a disgrace that that David Cameron is not here tonight to defend his record (.)
5		[but I want to see (3) I (4)]
6	Aud:	[APPLAUSE 7 seconds]
7	NS:	I want to see the Tories replaced with something better (.) when Ed talks about
8		cuts outside the protected areas that's jargon (.) let me tell you what that means
9		(.) that means cuts to social care (.) to social security to local government
10		services (.) to defence (.) Ed's in the position that's he's so thirled to austerity (.)
11		so scared to be bold that he's not even doing the right thing by the NHS he's not
12		promising the money the National Health Service needs (.) I think it's time not
13		for a pretend alternative to austerity (.)it's time for a real alternative to austerity
14		that's what I'm offering (.) and if Labour won't be bold enough on its own I think
15		people should vote for parties that will hold Labour to account and make them
16		bolder
17	Aud:	APPLAUSE 6 seconds
18	DD:	Nat Natalie Bennett (.) you were (.) you were nodding in agreement while she
19		was talking=
20	NB:	=exactly right (.) let's talk about one group of people (.) there are eight hundred
21		thousand people over the age of sixty-five in Britain at the moment (.) who need
22		social care who aren't getting it (turn continues)

The initial question is once again framed in terms of an opposition between two participants, Sturgeon and Miliband. However, Sturgeon avoids answering the conducive yes/no question by proposing an alternative frame, ignoring the previous exchange between Miliband and Farage about the details of the supposed spending cuts, widening the argument to restate her main political goal ('I want to get rid of the Tories'), and attacking David Cameron for not attending the debate (line 4). Sturgeon's reply is a 'dispreferred' response (Pomerantz and Heritage 2012), and as is typical of dispreferred moves, it is linguistically marked by the discourse marker 'well', a pause, and a false start on 'I' before the dispreferred response is given. This also signals what Goffman (1981: 128) describes as a change in 'footing', which 'implies a change in the alignment we take up to ourselves and others present as expressed in the way we manage the production and reception of an utterance'. This shift is also recognized by the audience who applaud for the first time in the debate. The applause is sustained for seven seconds and is a significant reaction, breaking up Sturgeon's reply. Sturgeon goes on to criticize Miliband, accusing Labour of not offering a 'real alternative to austerity'. She concludes the turn by setting out the SNP's influence on Labour to 'make them bolder' (lines 15 and 16), gaining a further six seconds of applause.

This extract does not include any uninvited contributions, but what it illustrates is another means by which power may be gained in a debate, namely the strategic use of metadiscourse (Ilie 2003). Here, and throughout the debates, the leaders refer to and reframe the contributions of their opponents in order to construct oppositional stances. For example, Sturgeon reframes Miliband's previous claims in the debate by saying: 'when Ed talks about cuts outside some protected areas that's jargon (.) let me tell you what that means (.) that means cuts to social care (.) to social security (.)' (lines 8 and 9). She explicitly reinterprets Miliband's contribution, downgrading it by referring to it as 'jargon' and describing his plans as 'pretend austerity'.

The next turn is allocated to Natalie Bennett, who expresses agreement with Sturgeon's prior contribution before taking a fifty-second turn in which she outlines the effects of spending cuts on social care, and sets out the Green Party's plans for creating more jobs in social care and the NHS (National Health Service). The end of her turn also receives applause. The moderator then allocates the next turn to Leanne Wood, by simply naming her rather than posing a particular premise or question. Wood describes the 'high price' of austerity, finishing her turn with a direct question to Ed Miliband, shown in Extract 4 that follows:

Extract 4

1	LW:	so if you were Prime Minister Ed I wonder if you could tell us would you be
2		prepared to hold (.) an eme<u>rg</u>ency budget to re<u>ver</u>se those Tory spending cuts
3		that are causing <u>so</u> much pain to <u>so</u> many people in <u>so</u> many of our communities
4	EM:	well⌈I you've given me a real opportunity Leanne (4)⌉
5	Aud:	⌊APPLAUSE 5 seconds ⌋
6	EM:	let me <u>tell</u> you what's going to be in Labour's first budget (.) we're going to have a
7		<u>man</u>sion tax on properties above two million pounds to fund our National Health
8		Service (.) something David Cameron would <u>never</u> do (.) we're going to a<u>bol</u>ish
9		the bedroom tax (.) we're going to have a bank <u>bonus</u> tax to put our young people
10		right across every part of the United Kingdom back to <u>work</u> (.) and I do say to to
11		some of the people on the stage tonight (.) let's not pretend there's <u>no</u> difference
12		between me and David Cameron you <u>know</u> Nicola there's a <u>huge</u> difference
13		between me and David Cameron (.)
14		just ⌈the three things I've mentioned ⌉and <u>so</u> many other things
15	NS:	⌊I'm going to make you bolder Ed⌋
16	EM:	besides⌈(.) and look the real ⌉danger in this country is of
17	NS:	⌊I'm just going to make you bolder⌋
18	EM:	a re-elected David Cameron who <u>doub</u>les the spending cuts (.) <u>fall</u>ing living
19		standards and a threat to our National Health Service and that is the big choice
20		on offer at this election=
		--
21	DD:	⌈=but Nicola is saying you should be bolder you may not have heard she said⌉
22	LW:	⌊=will you reverse his cuts re<u>ver</u>se his cuts will you reverse the⌈Tory's cuts⌉⌋
23	NS:	⌊I I don't say⌋

---

24   DD: you should be ⌈bolder ⌉

25   NS: ⌊I don't⌋ say=

26   NS: =there's no difference between=

27   =Ed Miliband and David⌈Cameron (.) I say there is not=⌉

28   EM: ⌊well that's good (.) that's a start⌋

29   NS: =a big enough difference between Ed Miliband (.)⌈and David⌉Cameron

30   NB: ⌊exactly ⌋

31   Aud: ⌈APPLAUSE 6 seconds   ⌉

32   NS: ⌊that's that's the thing now (.) Charlotte's (.)⌋

33   NS: Charlotte's question was rightly about the next generation (.) you know we have

34   experts saying (.) that if we continue with austerity cuts by twenty-twenty there

35   are going to be one million more children across the UK (.) living in poverty (.)

36   that would be a betrayal of the next generation (.) what I am proposing is

37   responsible (.) modest spending increases that still gets the deficit down because

38   yes that is important (.) but doesn't do it by heaping more and more pain onto

39   the backs of the people who can least afford it (.) and I want to say to Ed (.) we

40   share a desire to see the back of the Tories but surely (.) we don't want to replace

41   the Tories with Tory lite (.)

42   ED: and that's not⌈going to ⌉

43   NS: ⌊we need to⌋replace the Tories with something better

44   Aud: APPLAUSE 6 seconds

Wood ends her turn (lines 1–3) by effectively nominating Miliband to speak—a proposal the moderator could overrule, but does not. Miliband attempts to turn this to his advantage. As with Farage's question in Extract 2, he benefits from what is intended to be a challenge, evading Wood's question and instead using his turn to promote his own agenda at some length (lines 6–20). However, Sturgeon interrupts this twice, returning to her previous accusation that Labour 'are not bold enough' by saying 'I'm going to make you bolder.' These interruptions are not immediately successful; Miliband continues until both the moderator and Wood speak simultaneously at the end of his turn. Wood's intervention fails, but Dimbleby picks up Sturgeon's accusation, stating ironically 'you may not have heard' (line 21). But while Dimbleby is inviting Miliband to respond, Sturgeon interrupts him, responding directly to Miliband's claim that there are differences between him and Cameron by saying that the differences are not big enough (lines 25–29). Natalie Bennett takes a rare UN to support this comment by saying 'exactly' (line 30). Sturgeon's intervention is applauded by the audience. She goes on to say that they share a desire to 'see the back of the Tories' before accusing Miliband of being 'Tory lite' and demanding that the Tories are replaced with 'something better' (line 43). This again receives applause from the audience.

Extract 5 that follows is taken from the final part of the debate in response to the first question. Miliband attacks Sturgeon's economic plans for not being 'responsible' (lines 1–15); she unsuccessfully attempts to challenge him four times (lines 6, 9, 12, and 14) before saying 'let me ask you a direct question' (line 16). The moderator then defers the turn he has previously promised to Bennett to allow Sturgeon's question, which ends with the highly adversarial directive 'give us an answer' (line 24). Miliband interrupts (line 25) to claim that he has already made his position clear, but Sturgeon persists, her style reminiscent of a political interviewer as she interrupts to pin him down: 'how many billions?' (line 27):

Extract 5

1   EM: (end of turn) I think that the problem in our country is not that we are <u>one</u>

2   United Kingdom (.) it's that we're run for the richest and most powerful and we

3   should be run for working families again (.) and <u>my</u> plan does it but it's a

4   res<u>pon</u>sible plan Nicola (.) it's <u>not</u> a plan that denies we need to get the deficit

5   down (.) ⌜It's not a plan ⌝that denies=

6   NS: ⌞ hey b but what⌟

7   EM: =to Charlotte that we need to balance the books or people at home and people at

8   <u>home</u> know we have to live within our ⌜means ⌝

9   NS: ⌞ can I ⌟

10   ED: and you can come along on the stage tonight (.) and deny the need for difficult

11   decisions⌜and then plan seven point six⌝ billion pounds (.)

12   NS: ⌞ let me ask you a question Ed ⌟

13   EM: ⌜ worth of cuts in Scotland⌝(.)

14   NS: ⌞ let me ask you a direct ⌟

15   EM: but I don't think it is⌜ going to convince anyone⌝

16   NS: ⌞Ed Let me ask you a di<u>rect</u> question⌜y y you ⌝

17   DD: ⌞ a a alright⌟ Natalie

18   DD: and then'll come to you (.)

19   NS: you you quote the IFS at <u>me</u> the IFS said about <u>you</u> that if people vote Labour

20   they don't <u>know</u> what they're <u>voting</u> for now we <u>know</u> you voted with the Tories

21   for thirty billion pounds of cuts (.) you say that is <u>not</u> your plan but there will be

22   <u>cuts</u> (.) tell us tonight because people have a right to <u>know</u> (.) what is the <u>scale</u> of

23   the cut (.) how <u>much</u> cut are you talking about and where is the axe going to <u>fall</u>

24   it's a <u>simple</u> ⌜question (.) give us an <u>answer</u>⌝

25   EM: ⌞ I I've explained I've explained⌟ I've explained that outside the

26   protected areas (.) health education (.)⌜international⌝

27   NS: ⌞ how many ⌟ <u>billions</u>

While all the party leaders contribute to this 'free-flowing' part of the debate using a combination of invited and uninvited turns, Sturgeon's persistence in attacking Miliband is particularly fruitful. Starting with the change in footing in Extract 3, she develops a sustained attack, supported by Wood and Bennett, who share the same political stance on spending cuts. This stretch of discourse is dominated by the exchanges between Sturgeon and Miliband, even though the opposition was initially set up between Farage and Miliband. Though Sturgeon makes some use of UNs to put herself in this position, she is also facilitated by the moderator, who allows her to take and hold the floor and, on occasion, reiterates her points. Julie Etchingham, the moderator in the ITV debate, used a similar approach to enable direct engagement between Cameron and Miliband. In each case, the 'head-to-head' exchange between two participants dominated the proceedings for a sustained period.

It appears, then, that a participant's power on this multiparty debate floor is significantly boosted by his or her inclusion in dyadically structured 'head-to-head' exchanges, which function like mini-debates within the debate, and which typically unfold with the active support of the moderator. Once again, the leaders of the main parties are typically at an advantage here, because their contest is seen as the central contest in the election as a whole. Leanne Wood could (and in fact, did) make adversarial interventions and take UNs, but her position as leader of Plaid Cymru, a party unlikely to play more than a minor supporting role in any coalition because of its limited representation at Westminster, meant that her efforts to gain a foothold did not receive support. Sturgeon and Farage were treated as more significant players in this context because both represented significant threats to Miliband's chances of forming a majority Labour government. In the particular circumstances of the 'Challengers' debate', where Miliband's most significant rival (David Cameron) was absent, Sturgeon and Farage were in competition for the role of his main adversary—a role which, as Adams (2015: 221) has pointed out, confers significant interactional benefits. The question put to Ed Miliband to kick off the 'free-flowing' debate on government spending may suggest that the moderator initially considered Farage the obvious choice for the 'main adversary' role. But in the event, that role was taken by Sturgeon, who was able to sustain her attack not only through her own strategic moves, but also because the two other participants, Bennett and Wood, used their turns to reinforce her position. By contrast, Farage had no one to side with him against Miliband, and he was not able to regain the floor for long enough to build substantially on his earlier contribution.

In this section we have presented a descriptive analysis of the way participants in the second TV debate gained and made use of the floor. In the next section we will use the observations already made to address the question of whether women in leadership positions have a different style of speaking from men. As we noted in Chap. 1, discussions of this issue (both 'folk' and expert) frequently oppose the adversarial and competitive style said to be typical of men to the more consensual, cooperative, and supportive speech style allegedly favoured by women. We will therefore examine the use made by participants of the linguistic strategies and features that are typically cited in connection with these opposing styles.

Adversarial and Supportive Speech

The debate is inherently an adversarial genre, and it is already clear from the extracts reproduced above that all participants in the GE2015 debates made use of adversarial linguistic strategies such as bidding for the floor without invitation, interrupting other speakers, challenging other speakers' statements, reframing prior contributions in critical terms, and using directive speech acts without mitigation to put opponents on the spot (like Farage's 'tell me how you're going to balance the books?' in Extract 2 and Wood's 'will you reverse the Tories' cuts?' in Extract 4). In these debates, as in the debates analysed by Shaw (2000) in research on the House of Commons, both men and women used these strategies. The most significant gender difference noted by Shaw was women's greater attentiveness to the rules governing debates, and their avoidance of strategies which were defined as violations of the rules, such as interjecting comments from a sitting position. It is of interest to ask whether the same tendency for men to engage in 'disorderly' behaviour, and for women to avoid it, is observable in the televised election debates.

One kind of disorderly behaviour that occurs on numerous occasions during the two debates is continuing to speak in defiance of the moderator's instructions to cede the floor to another speaker. This directly challenges the moderator's authority, and also impinges on other speakers' rights by cutting into their speaking time. It was particularly common in the ITV debate, which contained forty-two instances of participants continuing to speak after they had been told to stop (in the BBC debate, there were only eleven such instances). Here, we will focus on an example, transcribed next as Extract 6, which is particularly interesting because some of those involved explicitly orient to gender difference as a relevant issue.

These references to gender occurred during the final 'free-flowing' segment of the ITV debate, responding to a question from a twenty-five-year-old graduate who had asked: 'what will you do for my generation to help us feel optimistic about our future?' This section of the discussion is dominated by David Cameron, Ed Miliband, and Nick Clegg. It begins with Cameron attacking Miliband, at which point Clegg interrupts Cameron to accuse him of 'planning to cut money for schools'. Cameron then accuses Clegg of taking a 'pick and mix' approach to the coalition's policies, saying 'Nick Clegg we sat in the cabinet room together, we took difficult decisions together', casting Clegg as an inconsistent and untrustworthy partner. Miliband takes advantage of this discord by saying they are 'blaming each other and they're both right' before attacking both of them. The sequence reproduced next starts when Clegg responds to Miliband's accusation that he broke his promises about university tuition fees and 'betrayed the young people of our country':

Extract 6

1	NC:	I mean you know I get this sort of pious er <u>stan</u>ce from Ed Miliband (.) this is the
2		<u>man</u> (.) who was part of a <u>gov</u>ernment that said no boom and bust in the
3		economy (.) and <u>crash</u>ed our economy (.) <u>jeo</u>pardizing the future generations
4		and life chances of <u>mil</u>lions of people in this country (.) I have a<u>pol</u>ogized (.) I
5		have taken responsibility for the mistakes I've made why don't you in <u>front</u> of the
6		British people Ed Miliband a<u>pol</u>ogise for ⌈your role in crashing ⌉(.) <u>no</u> no not <u>say</u>=
7	EM:	⌊we <u>said</u> we got it we s⌋

8	NC:	=nothing euphe<u>mis</u>tic (.) say I'm <u>sorry</u> for ⌈crashing the British ⌉ economy=
9	Em:	⎨ of course we said ⎬
10	JE:	⌊Ed Miliband Ed Miliband⌋

11	EM:	=of course ⌈we said we got it <u>wrong</u> on bank regulation (.) absolutely⌉ we said we
12	Aud:	⌊APPLAUSE 4 seconds ⌋
13	EM:	we said sorry for what we did in relation to the banks and the banks <u>were</u> under-
14		regulated ⌈but let me just point ⌉this out=
15	DC:	⎨ but Ed it's not just ⎬
16	JE:	⌊<u>thank</u> you David ⌋
17	EM:	=there was a global financial crisis let just point this out (.) David when <u>you</u> were
18		in opposition at the time as leader of the opposition you were saying the banks
19		were <u>over</u>-regulated (.) so I'm really not going to take any lectures from <u>you</u>
20		about the global financial <u>cri</u>sis

21	Aud:	⌈laughter and applause 4 seconds ⌉
22	DC:	{ Ed Miliband (.) Ed Miliband= }
23	JE:	⌊Thank you gentlemen thank you I'm going to⌋

| 24 | DC: | ⌈=still thinks the last government didn't <u>borr</u>ow enough=⌉ |
| 25 | JE: | ⌊thank you thank you thank you gentleman I'm going to ⌋ |

26 DC: =didn't ⌈<u>spend</u>⌉ enough didn't <u>tax</u> enough I mean <u>that</u> is the truth and young

27 NS: ⌊ er ⌋

28 DC: people suffer the most when you have an economy (.) with out-of-control welfare

29 out-of-control debt out-of-control spending (.) <u>young</u> people suffer the most

30 because the <u>deficit</u> (.) and the <u>debt</u> is on <u>their</u> ⌈heads for future generations⌉

31 EM: ⌊ no they⌈ suffer the most ⌋

32 JE: ⌊okay thank you ⌋

----

33 EM: ⌈when you have a Con<u>ser</u>vative Prime Minister making <u>un</u>fair choices (.) ⌉

34 JE: ⌊thank you thank you very much indeed Ed Miliband thank you Natalie Bennett⌋

----

35 EM: <u>that</u>'s why they suffer ⌈David ⌉

36 JE: ⌊<u>thank</u> you ⌋ Natalie <u>Ben</u>nett

37 NB: I think we <u>were</u> talking about edu<u>ca</u>tion (.)

38 NS: ex<u>ac</u>tly *laughs*

----

39 Aud: ⌈laughter 1 sec ⌉

40 NB: { so perhaps we }can go back there (.)

41 NF: ⌊why *unclear* ⌋

42 NB: and to come back to the point about education and particularly the point that

43 David Cameron raised about free schools (turn continues)

This markedly adversarial exchange starts with Clegg's directive to Ed Miliband to 'say I'm sorry for crashing the economy' (lines 5–8). Miliband defends his position and attacks Cameron for his previous position that the banks were 'over-regulated' (lines 17–20), which is greeted with laughter and applause by the audience. Cameron then retaliates, ignoring Etchingham's instructions to finish speaking. She responds by addressing not just Cameron but the 'gentlemen' taking part in this exchange. However, Cameron continues with his turn and Etchingham temporarily suspends her attempts to stop him.

Etchingham's use of the gendered term 'gentlemen' underlines that it is men, rather than women, who are breaking the rules, but perhaps also that it is mainly the women who are being prevented from speaking by the men's behaviour. It is clear from Nicola Sturgeon's reaction that she feels excluded from this section of the debate. She laughs and shakes her head when the moderator is ignored, and at the point where Cameron defies instructions to stop speaking, she starts to intervene (line 27). Her critical stance is also captured in the visual representation of this sequence for the television audience: the camera cuts away to Sturgeon twice in this segment, showing a reaction shot in which her expression is one of disgruntled amusement. When the moderator regains control, the next turn is allocated to Bennett, who refers obliquely to the previous disorderly conduct by saying 'I think we were talking about education', marking the previous exchanges as a digression from the original question. Sturgeon agrees by saying 'exactly' and laughing (line 38). The next turn goes to Wood, who refers to the Welsh education system, then the following turn is allocated to Sturgeon, who alludes to the disorderly conduct of the men by saying: 'Well I-I think we've seen tonight from this discussion why we really need to break the old boys' network at Westminster.'

Sturgeon's use of the gendered description 'old boys' network at Westminster' is interesting, since it taps into what Chap. 3 will show is a common folk linguistic ideology, much used in media commentary on the debates, which contrasts female politicians' supposed 'different voice' with the familiar voice of the 'male political establishment'. Rhetorically, this contrast tends to work to the advantage of the women, representing their way of doing politics as both more 'modern' and less off-putting to the public than the traditional male approach. It is possible Sturgeon is exploiting this deliberately and strategically, since this is the only point in either debate where any leader constructs an opponent (and by implication, therefore, herself) in specifically gendered terms. In her study of US televised debates, Adams (2015: 240) also noted that 'the direct indexing of gender and selection of a gendered situated identity was not a dominant strategy'. When it does occur, therefore, we may suspect that it is serving a strategic purpose—in this case, enabling a female speaker to make what is potentially a highly adversarial move, an attack on her male opponents, by mobilizing the popular belief that women do not engage in such attacks.

In reality, women—like men—may behave in ways which are not only adversarial but markedly aggressive. An example occurs during the BBC debate when Miliband and Farage engage in a lengthy argument about UKIP's position on the privatization of the NHS. In the sequence reproduced next, the moderator David Dimbleby is mainly concerned with regulating the topic of the debate (which is not, at this point, the NHS), but he also appears to prioritize Ed Miliband's entitlement to hold the floor over Natalie Bennett's right to take her turn. Bennett attempts to gain the floor by shouting loudly that it is her turn to speak. This is an extremely aggressive intervention—the only case in either debate where a politician raises their voice to this extent—and it does not immediately bring the Miliband–Farage confrontation to a close:

Extract 7

1 EM: (end of turn) people at home need to know this (.) you don't <u>want</u> the National

2   Health Service you want a <u>priv</u>ate insurance system of healthcare (.) you've said

3   it on the <u>rec</u>ord (.)

----

4 EM: ⌜ you've ⌝ said ⌠ you want to re<u>tur</u>n to it (.) that's your real agenda which is ⌝

5 NB: ⌊ Ed ⌋ ⎰ now just to come in on something something that you ⎱

6 DD: ⌊ alright Ed Miliband wait wait wait (.) wait wait wait ⌟

----

7 NB: Ed Miliband=

8 EM: =that's your real agenda⌠ and you will support   ⌝David Cameron with <u>his</u>=

9 NF   ⎰ can I just say   ⎰

10 DD: ⌊ alright alright now hold on⌟

----

11 EM: =plans to ⌐ privatise the National Health Service   ⌝

12 NF: ⎮ I'm not having that (.) I'm not having that= ⎮

13 DD: ⎮ alright (.) we are not no no   ⎮

14 NB: ⌊ Ed Miliband Miliband   ⌟

----

15 NF: =you can<u>not</u> conduct this⌠ debate ⌝

16 DD: ⌊ Nigel] ⌟ can you just pause for a moment we're <u>not</u>

17   debating the NHS (.) alright=

18 NF: =well I'd like to answer him on that <u>please</u>=

19 DD: =w well you can have one <u>brief</u> answer and then we must move on=

20 NF: =stop LYING (.) UKIP believes in the National Health Service (.) free at the point

---

21   of ⌈delivery it was you it was you=
22 EM: ⌊okay David I must come back ⌈on⌉that because he accused me of lying ⌋
23 NB: ⌊no⌋

---

24 NF: =that privatised ⌈a large chunk of the health ⌈service and=⌉
25 EM: ⌊I want to come back on you⌊and this is= ⌋
26 NB: ⌊no it's my ⌋

---

27 NF: ⌈=you are lying and ⌈ you are lying to millions and millions=   ⌉
28 EM: ⌊=what you said Nigel⌊this is what you said this is what you said   ⌋
29 NB: ⌊ED I BELIEVE IT IS MY TURN TO COME IN NOW   ⌋

---

30 NF: =of people and⌈ and you keep on doing it and=⌉
31 DD: ⌊Nat Natalie   ⌋

---

32 NF: ⌈=lying won't win ⌈you the election⌉
33 DD: ⌊you made the point⌊you've made   ⌊the point of course if you've been=
34 Aud: ⌊Shouting   ⌋

---

35 DD: =accused of lying ⌈you have the right to reply   ⌉
36 EM: ⌊I think Natalie wanted to come ⌋in David
37 DD: I thought you wanted to come in=
38 EM: =I did but

39   DD: =okay Natalie briefly (.)

40   NB: I think it was <u>probably</u> my <u>turn</u> (.) I do want to say something to you Ed that you

41   are on the record about (.) you're comfortable with a five percent private

42   profit for private companies operating in the NHS (.)

----

43   DD: Alright ⌈Ed ⌉

44   NB: ⌊we⌋ should have <u>zero</u> ⌈percent profit in the NHS   ⌉

45   EM: ⌊I just want to come back on this point⌋

----

46   Aud: ⌈APPLAUSE 3 seconds⌉

47   DD: ⌊alright this is the last⌋ the last point please=

----

48   ⌈=as I said we won't continue debating this⌉

49   EM: ⌊Ni-Nigel this is what you've said   ⌋"I think we are going to have to move

50   to an insurance-based system" (turn continues)

In this extract both Bennett and Farage engage in forms of adversarial linguistic behaviour that fall outside the accepted norms of political debate. Bennett tries to shout her way onto the floor and Farage accuses another politician of lying (this flouts a convention derived from Parliamentary rules, which specifically prohibit calling other members liars). In Farage's case this is part of a pattern of non-normative behaviour. In the first, ITV debate, he made controversial claims about 'health tourism' and HIV which drew immediate censure from Wood and then Sturgeon. In the BBC debate, he accused the audience of being 'left-wing', a bizarrely self-destructive move that prompted Miliband to comment, 'It's never a good idea to attack the audience, Nigel.' Bennett's shouting during this sequence, by contrast, is not typical of her behaviour overall. But in comparison with the others, both she and Farage often appear unsophisticated. Bennett's behaviour shows that 'extreme' rule-breaking is not an exclusively male preserve, but it also underlines, as does Farage's, that the most effective debaters are not those who flout the rules most aggressively but those who pursue their goals in subtler ways.

Sturgeon and Wood both show the ability to do this, even though they, like Bennett and Farage, lack the interactional advantages which accrue to Cameron, Clegg, and Miliband by virtue of their roles as government and opposition leaders. Wood, for instance, manages to make herself heard by taking a speaking turn immediately after the moderator has allocated it to someone else:

Extract 8

1	NC:	(end of turn) I don't equally think it is <u>fair</u> (.) to do what the Labour party want to
2		do (.) which is actually to increase <u>bor</u>rowing that doesn't <u>help</u> the future
3		generation=
4	JE:	=let's put that point ⌈directly to Ed Miliband⌉
5	LW:	⌊but the the <u>way</u> the ⌋<u>way</u> that you've done it so <u>far</u> (.)
6		you've been balancing the books on the backs of the <u>poor</u> (.)
7		⌈seventy-nine thousand⌉
8	NC:	⌊ no we've actually ⌋done it
9	NC:	⌈in a <u>bal</u>anced way⌉
10	LW:	⌊seventy nine ⌋thousand ⌈people ⌉
11	NF:	⌊the books⌋aren't <u>bal</u>anced=
12	NF:	⌈=we've got a ninety billion <u>deficit=</u>⌉
13	LW:	⌊seventy-nine thousand people ⌋
14	NF:	=I mean what's going <u>on</u> here can we GET REAL PLEASE
15	Aud:	⌈laughter 1 second⌉
16	JE:	⌈thank <u>thank</u> you⌉
17	NC:	⌊the deficit ⌋is <u>halved</u> it is <u>halved</u>=
18	NF:	=no it <u>hasn't</u> it has⌈virtually <u>doubled</u>⌉
19	LW:	⌊seventy-nine ⌋thousand people ⌈are reliant on food banks⌉
20	JE:	⌊thank you Ed Miliband⌋
21	LW:	thirty percent of young people in my
22		⌈constituency of the Rhondda are unem<u>ployed</u> ⌉
23	JE:	⌊Leanne Wood thank you Ed Miliband thank you⌋

Here, Clegg's first turn is a criticism directed at Miliband, and in a move we have identified as characteristic of these debates, the moderator allocates the next turn to Miliband so that he can respond directly. However, Wood interrupts and hijacks the speaking turn to put her own point to Clegg (line 5). Having gained the floor, she continues to speak despite competition from Farage, and is able to deliver her point about food banks in her constituency.

Wood also stands out as the only speaker to use a 'secure' speaking turn interactively to challenge an opponent. In the BBC debate, Wood used the slot she was given following the fourth question from the audience, on immigration, to attack Nigel Farage. Farage's turn directly preceded Wood's, and she began with a comment on what he had just said: 'so you abuse immigrants and those with HIV and then complain that UKIP is being abused'. This won applause from the audience, after which she resumed her turn. Secure turns are opportunities for pre-planned and rehearsed statements, so Wood's improvised response to the previous turn showed she was sufficiently confident to stray from her script. None of the other speakers did this. Bennett, the least experienced participant, appeared particularly dependent on a pre-prepared script, and rarely related her arguments to the previous or ongoing discussion.

Nicola Sturgeon also showed the ability to adopt adversarial positions and assert her claims to the floor without using 'crude' strategies which would alienate her audience. We noted earlier that she was able to gain a substantial share of the speaking time despite being allocated relatively few turns by the moderator, and that she achieved this by taking UNs (examples are given in our discussion of Extracts 4 and 5). She also resisted attempts by the moderator to cut off points she had not finished making. Her interventions often took the form of challenges to her opponents, but these were delivered in a calm and composed manner, without the heated quality of the exchanges we have examined between Miliband, Clegg, and Cameron (Extracts 6 and 7) or the shouting to which Farage and Bennett sometimes resorted (Extract 8).

Another 'subtle' strategy that Sturgeon used effectively was manipulating 'key' (Hymes 1972), shifting from a serious tone to a mocking, ironic, or humorous one. In her first turn in the ITV debate (immediately after the exchange between Clegg, Cameron, and Miliband in Extract 1), she began:

Extract 9

1	NS:	It's really i<u>roni</u>c isn't it hearing Nick Clegg and David Cameron argue when they
2		have been hand in glove imposing austerity on the people of this country (.) for
3		the last five years (.) David said in his opening remarks that everybody apart
4		from him had been proved <u>wrong</u> (.) over the past five years that's actually <u>not</u>
5		the case er David Cameron has missed his own borrowing targets by a <u>hund</u>red-
6		and-fifty <u>billi</u>on pounds (.) his <u>poli</u>cies are pushing children into <u>poverty</u> (turn
7		continues)

Here, Sturgeon starts with a metalinguistic statement, recasting the previous exchanges to underline Clegg and Cameron's inconsistency and guiding the audience to interpret it in a particular way. The statement and question tag 'it's ironic, isn't it?' is inclusive in that it invites the rest of the panel and the studio and viewing audiences to agree with the statement. Sturgeon also accompanies her criticism with a 'laughing voice' on the words 'imposing austerity on the people of this country'. This laughter, produced while speaking, is characteristic of Sturgeon's public voice at First Minister's Question Time in the Scottish Parliament; she also used it in some one-to-one broadcast interviews during the campaign. In context, it can serve a number of strategic purposes. On the one hand, it can express scorn and ridicule: in the previous extract, it highlights the ludicrousness of a staged argument between two leaders who have been 'hand in glove'—that is, part of a governing coalition—for the previous five years. On the other hand, it has a mitigating function: it allows Sturgeon to couch her attack on the coalition partners in a friendly, conspiratorial tone which positions the audience as allies.

Sturgeon also used humour to oppose other politicians, particularly Farage. In the ITV debate, she made a joke out of Farage's views on immigration:

Extract 10

1   NS: Well the NHS budget in Scotland has increased by three billion pounds since the

2   SNP took office (.) ⌈ so It will go ⌉ up by four hundred million pounds (.) next

3   NC: ⌊ less than here ⌋

4   NS: year (.) you know look I I I actually think well one of the things that we've

5   learned is that there's not anything that Nigel Farage won't blame

6   on foreigners ⌈ er actually   ⌉

7   Aud: ⌊ laughter 1 second ⌋

8   NS: the pressures on our health service (.) many of them are things we should

9   celebrate (.) people are living longer (turn continues)

Here, Sturgeon inserts a humorous attack on Farage in the middle of her turn; the hesitations, discourse markers, and hedges in lines 4–6 may indicate that this is a spontaneous reframing of her argument in the light of Farage's earlier comments. The humour of the comment that 'there's not anything that Nigel Farage won't blame on foreigners' is produced by hyperbole, and this is effective in eliciting laughter from the audience. Sturgeon also uses the strategies other researchers have categorized as 'wisecracks' and 'asides', and which have often been associated with masculine styles of public speaking. For example, in the same debate, she produces an aside directed at Farage:

Extract 11

1   JE: thank you Nigel ⌈Farage   ⌉

2   NF: ⌊my challenge⌋ to everyone here was of course er ignored and

3   brushed aside for chiefly ⌈ politically correct ⌉ reasons (.) Terry wants to

4   NS: ⌊ back to the point   ⌋

5   NF: know where the money is coming from and yes you've got to put money in

6   you've got to stop money being wasted (.) I mentioned health tourism (turn

7   continues)

The parenthetical comment 'back to the point' is intended to undermine Farage by implying that his political agenda is limited and irrelevant.

In the BBC debate, Sturgeon used humour more extensively. Extract 12 shows her employing sarcasm in the suggestion that Farage is trying to 'win friends and influence people' (line 5), which refers both to his position on immigration and to the charge of left-wing bias which he has levelled against the BBC audience. When he starts to respond with 'it's astonishing', she ridicules him with 'you are yes'. Both moves elicit laughter from the audience:

Extract 12

1 NS: (end of turn) we need to <u>build</u> more <u>hou</u>ses (.)

2 NF: right

3 NS: sub<u>stan</u>tially more houses and then we need to prot<u>ect</u> them for the people who

4   <u>can't</u> buy their own home and need to <u>rent</u> (.) now you know Nigel I you are

5   obviously on a setting out to win friends and <u>in</u>fluence people tonight (.) but if

6   we can get a<u>way</u> (.)

----

7 Aud: ⎧ laughter 2 seconds   ⎫

8 NS: ⎩ but if we can get a<u>way</u> ⎭ in this de<u>bate</u> (.) from the idea that <u>every</u> problem in

9 NF: ⎩ so (.) so ⎭

----

10 NS: this country is caused by immigrants (.) you know immigrants from the

11   European Union into this country make a net contri<u>bution</u> to our country so if we

12   can maybe just (.) put the <u>bog</u>eyman to one side we can actually <u>deb</u>ate these

13   issues (.) for <u>real</u> and in <u>sub</u>stance (.)

14 Aud: ⎧APPLAUSE   6 seconds   ⎫

15 DD: ⎨ uh um can I⎤ can can I (.) sorry can I just alert you all to the ⎭ fact you

16 NF: ⎩I I I just ⎭

17 DD: don't <u>know</u> the questions that are coming (.) I <u>do</u> and there <u>is</u> a question coming

18   on immigration so let's perhaps not go into <u>too</u> much depth on that for the

19   ⎧moment⎤

20 NF: ⎩yeah it's ⎭ just as<u>ton</u>ishing (.) if you er if you⎧cannot accept⎤ if you cannot accept

21 NS: ⎩ you <u>are</u> yes ⎭

22 AUD: Laughter 2 seconds

Asides and wisecracks are also part of Farage's own debate style, but the effect tends to vary: he is good at eliciting laughter when he makes jokes at the expense of what he calls 'the politically correct political class' (we return to this aspect of his performance in Chap. 4), but he can also alienate the audience with comments like the ones Sturgeon takes aim at. His uninvited interventions are not always effective: some of the briefer ones (like the ironic 'yups' in Extract 2, which resemble minimal responses in spontaneous conversations) are too informal and 'non-debate-like' (Edelsky and Adams 1990) to communicate a substantive challenge to their target. By contrast, as one media commentator observed (see Chap. 3), Sturgeon generally 'lands [her] punches'. Her use of humour shows her as a skilful communicator who can manipulate key to produce a range of effects and audience responses.

While political debates are, as we observed above, inherently adversarial speech events, cooperative and supportive behaviour may also serve important purposes, particularly in the context of a multiparty debate. Where an exchange is not simply a head-to-head confrontation between two opposing candidates, individuals may make a tactical choice to align themselves with some of their co-participants as a way of strengthening their position vis-à-vis others. These alliances may be temporary and shifting, reflecting moment-to-moment calculations by each participant about what will best serve their goals at a given point.

This tactical dimension typically goes unacknowledged by proponents of the 'different voice' ideology, in which women's use of cooperative and supportive strategies is seen as the result of a fixed, gender-based preference for a certain style of speaking. This view was regularly expressed in the media commentary on the debates which we discuss in more detail in Chap. 3. Commentators were well aware that Sturgeon, Wood, and Bennett were political allies, united by their opposition to the austerity policies which all the main parties (and UKIP) supported. Nevertheless, the support the three women gave one another was most frequently interpreted in gendered terms. Much was made, for instance, of their symbolic 'group hug' at the end of the BBC debate, but this was typically presented not as a gesture of solidarity among political allies but as an act of female bonding. The group hug may, of course, have been both of those things, but our analysis of the debate itself suggests that cooperative and supportive verbal strategies were most often used, by both sexes, for tactical reasons.

To illustrate the tactical use of supportive moves, we will turn to another extract from the 'disorderly' section of the ITV debate, in which the leaders are responding to the first question on government spending and austerity:

Extract 13

```
1    NS:   the canny Scots have paid more tax per head of population to the treasury in

2          every single year for the past thirty-four years (.) that's the reality but the

3          question for Ed Miliband Ed talks the language of anti-austerity but it's only a

4          few weeks since (.) Ed Miliband trooped though the lobbies of the House of

5          Commons with Nick Clegg (.) with David Cameron to vote for thirty billion

6          pounds of cuts⎡over ⎤the next two years (.) I take a different view=

7    NC:        ⎣ yes ⎦

8    NS:   =to that I don't believe you can simply cut your way out of deficit (.) I think David

9          Cameron has proved that (.) he's missed all of his borrowing targets we need to

10         invest and grow (.) our way out of the deficit we've got ⎡experts ⎤saying that

11   NC:              ⎣I think ⎦

12         ⎡austerity (.) has ⎤held back economic growth so let's have =

13   DC:   ⎣wait a minute ⎦

14   NS:   =spending increases (.) modest spending increases that allow us to invest in the

15         things that matter ⎡economic growth and protecting     ⎤ the vulnerable=

16   NC:              ⎣it is a skeleton in the same cupboard ⎦

17   EM:   =I want to come back directly to Nicola Sturgeon ⎡in fact no that's that th⎤

18   NS:                   ⎣why did you vote for= ⎦

19         =thirty billion pounds of cuts Ed=

20   EM:   =that th that wasn't what the vote was for=

     -------------------------------------------------------------------------------------------------

21   NC:   =yes ⎡it was⎤

22   NS:      ⎣yes it ⎦was=

23   DC:            =it was=
```

24   NF: =it was

----

25   EM: in fact just just two weeks ago we had a vote against against Tory austerity your SNP

26   MPs didn't turn up ⌈let me⌉let me just say to you Nicola

27   NS: ⌊but it⌋

----

28   EM: ⌈let me just say to you Nicola let me just say to you Nicola you've ⌈got a plan=⌉

29   NS: ⌊let me just let me Julie on that specific point⌈the reason ⌉   ⌈   ⌉

30   JE: ⌊no I I er⌋   ⌊thank you⌋

----

31   EM: =you've got a plan to cut six billion pounds

32   ⌈in Scotland the fiscal⌉economy plan and you need to

33   NS: ⌊the the only cuts   ⌋

34   EM: explain what that would mean for the people of

35   ⌈Scotland the reality is the SNP cuts are just the same as the ⌈Tory cuts ⌉

36   NS: ⌊the only cuts on the horizon are the cuts that Ed Miliband ⌊is making⌋

37   NB: ⌊Julie=   ⌋

38   NB: =Nicola Sturgeon is ⌈absolutely right   ⌉

39   NS: ⌊the only point in the anti- ⌋ austerity motion=

40   JE: ⌊thank you Nicola Sturgeon⌋

41   NS: ⌈=that Ed Miliband talks about⌉

42   JE: ⌊thank you Nicola Sturgeon   ⌋   thank you⌈Natalie Bennett⌉

43   NB: ⌊Nicola Sturgeon⌋ is absolutely

44   right (.) you have a choice in the two largest parties here between 'austerity-

45   heavy' and 'austerity-lite' (turn continues)

In this extract, it is of interest to consider both the relationship between two of the women, Natalie Bennett and Nicola Sturgeon, and the relationship between two of the men, David Cameron and Nick Clegg. In relation to Bennett and Sturgeon, the most interesting sequence begins at line 38.

Bennett takes a rare UN, appealing to the moderator before asserting that 'Nicola Sturgeon is absolutely right.' Sturgeon continues to speak, and the moderator attempts to bring her turn to an end by saying 'thank you Nicola Sturgeon' twice. She then allocates a turn to Bennett, who reiterates her agreement with Sturgeon and attacks Cameron's policies. This sequence demonstrates that rhetorical agreement between speakers does not rule out competition between them. The content of Bennett's UN is an explicit expression of support for Sturgeon, but it is also an interruption, an attempt to cut short Sturgeon's turn while drawing the moderator's attention to Bennett's own claim to the floor. Sturgeon responds in a 'competitive' rather than 'cooperative' way: rather than yielding to Bennett, she continues to hold the floor until the moderator repeatedly requests her to stop, and allocates the next turn to Bennett. Bennett gains not only a speaking turn, but also the advantage of being aligned with a speaker who has just mounted a sustained attack on their common adversary.

Though Cameron and Clegg generally position themselves as opponents in the debate (a point derisively pounced on by Sturgeon in Extract 9), in relation to the question under discussion, they have a shared interest in defending the record of the coalition government they formed together in 2010. However, Cameron appears unwilling to treat Clegg as an equal partner in this endeavour. In a directive which is only just audible, he tells Clegg to 'wait a minute' (line 13), presumably because he wants to respond to Sturgeon's charge that he has 'missed all his borrowing targets' himself rather than allowing Clegg to represent them both. This exposes the inherently hierarchical nature of their relationship: Clegg does not attempt to moderate Cameron's contributions in the same way.

It is also noticeable that four of the leaders—Clegg, Sturgeon, Cameron, and Farage—cooperate to signal disagreement with Miliband's claim that a recent House of Commons vote was not 'about thirty billion pounds of cuts', producing a series of consecutive, matched utterances ('Yes it was', lines 21–24). The speech act being performed here is adversarial (directly contradicting another speaker), but the strategies of echoing or recycling another speaker's words and timing the turn containing those words to follow immediately from the previous turn are both associated with cooperative and supportive speech. In this case, the cooperation is clearly tactical, and the alliance is temporary. The four leaders involved do not have a shared political stance on the general issue of government spending cuts, but at this juncture, it is in all their interests to band together in opposition to Miliband, constructing him as a weak leader whose actions are at odds with his words.

A Different Voice?

Overall, the analysis we have presented in this chapter does not support the belief that women do political leadership, or political communication, 'in a different voice'. The picture we have drawn of women's participation in the national TV debates which were the centrepiece of the GE2015 campaign is more complicated than that. It is a picture in which individual differences, and differences in role and status reflecting the position of a leader's political party, loom larger than gender differences as an influence on linguistic behaviour. It is also a picture in which male–female similarities appear more numerous than male–female differences.

All the leaders used adversarial discourse strategies, as might be expected in the context of a speech event billed as a 'debate'. Some individuals used them more frequently than others, and there was one notable outlier, Natalie Bennett, whose relative political inexperience seems to have limited her ability to use the full range of adversarial strategies (especially those which call for improvisation). Nevertheless, our analysis demonstrates that both male and female leaders made use of interruptions, direct questions whose function is to challenge the addressee rather than merely to seek information, accusations, critical and sometimes hyperbolic descriptions of opponents, and reformulations of an opponent's point which are designed to show it, and the opponent, in a negative light. Conversely, all the leaders used at least some cooperative, supportive, and 'relational' or rapport-building strategies. They all addressed the viewing audience directly as 'you' in opening and closing statements, and looked directly into the camera. Inclusive uses of 'we' were also common, as was addressing studio audience members who asked questions by name, a 're-keying' of political discourse towards a more personal, informal mode of address. According to Drake and Higgins (2012), these strategies were not used consistently by all leaders in 2010, when the televised debate was a new genre in British politics, but it seems they have now become conventionalized. The demands of the genre are complex, encouraging what Banwart and McKinney (2005) label 'gendered adaptiveness', a willingness to combine the traditionally 'masculine' norms of adversarial debate with 'feminine' communication styles which help to construct 'authenticity' and build rapport with the viewer at home.

In a case study such as this, it is necessary to be cautious when making claims about gender differences. Not only are we dealing with very small numbers of male and female politicians, they are also differentiated by characteristics other than gender. One such differentiating characteristic, which may have a particular bearing on debating styles, is membership or non-membership of the Westminster Parliament. Three of the four men were MPs, with extensive experience of the arcane and highly adversarial norms that govern debate in the House of Commons; Cameron and Miliband also had the more specific experience of confronting each other regularly in the ritual exchanges of Prime Minister's Questions. By contrast, the women had not previously been involved in regular public exchanges with any of their opponents. Natalie Bennett was not a member of any UK legislative body, while Nicola Bennett and Leanne Wood gained their skills and experience in the Scottish Parliament and Welsh Assembly, respectively. This may help to explain why the female leaders showed less animosity in head-to-head exchanges than those who were members of what Nicola Sturgeon called 'the old boys' network at Westminster' (though we will see in Chap. 4 that on her home territory, in the Scottish Parliament, First Minister Sturgeon is capable of highly combative exchanges with her own Leader of the Opposition).

Another point that differentiated men and women was that men made more reference to their family roles and relationships. Miliband told Leanne Wood during the ITV debate that 'both my sons were born in a PFI ['private finance initiative'] hospital'; in the same debate, Farage noted that 'the Farage family were foreigners once', to which Clegg responded: 'I'm married to a foreigner, you are married to a foreigner'. Men did not use this rhetorical strategy frequently, but it is notable that the women appeared to avoid it—perhaps because of the sexist double standard which judges men positively for their active involvement in family life, whereas in women, this is more likely to raise doubts about their competence or commitment. As we noted earlier, it was rare for women to make gender relevant at all: the example we discussed above, Nicola Sturgeon's reference to 'the old boys' network at Westminster', was, we suggested, a strategic move, involving a negative allusion to her opponents' gender rather than a direct invocation of her own.

One difference which we thought we might find, the greater male propensity to engage in rule-breaking which has been observed in other contexts, did not, in the event, manifest itself. None of the women behaved in the guarded, deferential, and meticulously rule-observant way which has been associated with the status of the 'interloper'. The format of the debates did not require that all participants be treated equally in terms of speaking time, and as leaders of smaller parties, the women undoubtedly lost out to higher-status participants in competition for the floor. However, it is instructive here to compare Nicola Sturgeon with Nigel Farage, the only man whose status was comparable to hers, in that both led parties which were small but potentially influential (whereas Bennett and Wood led parties whose potential influence was very limited). The figures presented earlier in this chapter show that Farage and Sturgeon were closely matched on measures of speaking time. In the first debate, Farage spoke for about half a minute more than Sturgeon, while in the second, she spoke for just over a minute longer than he did. In the first debate, they also secured almost the same number of invited turns (a measure which is of interest because it gives a rough indication of the moderator's assessment of each participant's standing). In the second debate, he secured significantly more invited turns than she did (nineteen to her ten), but we have already noted that the low number of turns allocated to Sturgeon on that occasion was probably related to her effectiveness in gaining the floor through uninvited interventions.

In summary, both female and male participants in the televised election debates spoke in a range of voices. Their performances had to meet both the demands of the political debate genre (in which participants win points for their authority and skill in argument) and the requirements of the televisual medium (which encourages dramatic confrontations, but also calls on performers to display sincerity, authenticity, and empathy for the viewer at home). To meet these demands, they drew on a communicative repertoire which included both strategies culturally coded as 'masculine' and strategies culturally coded as 'feminine'.

Before drawing any more general conclusions, however, it is necessary to acknowledge that the analysis we have presented here of the leaders' performances in debates does not tell the whole story. It is also important to consider the other side of the communication coin, the reception of their performances. The gendering of language is accomplished not only through speakers' own linguistic behaviour, but also through the assumptions and expectations which addressees may bring to bear on interpreting speakers' behaviour (Cameron 1997). Even if female politicians do not, objectively, speak 'in a different voice' from their male counterparts, they may still be constructed as different in representations of their speech. In the next chapter, therefore, we turn our attention to the way the female party leaders, and their linguistic performance in the debates, were represented by the British press.

REFERENCES

Adams, K. L. (1992). Accruing power on debate floors. In K. Hall, M. Bucholtz, & B. Moonwomon (Eds.), *Locating power: Proceedings of the second Berkeley women and language conference* (pp. 1–10). Berkeley, CA: Berkeley Women and Language Group.

Adams, K. L. (2015). Governors debating: The role of situational, discourse and transportable identities. In J. Wilson & D. Boxer (Eds.), *Discourse, politics and women as global leaders* (pp. 217–249). Amsterdam: John Benjamins Publishing Company.

Banwart, M. C., & McKinney, M. S. (2005). A gendered influence in campaign debates? Analysis of mixed-gender United States senate and gubernatorial debates. *Communication Studies, 56*(4), 353–373.

Baxter, J. (2010). *The language of female leadership*. London; New York, NY: Palgrave Macmillan.

Beckett, C. (2015). The battle for the stage: Broadcasting. In P. Cowley & D. Kavanagh (Eds.), *The British General Election of 2015* (pp. 278–301). Basingstoke, Hampshire: Palgrave Macmillan.

Cameron, D. (1997). Performing gender identity: Young men's talk and the construction of heterosexual masculinity. In S. Johnson & U. H. Meinhof (Eds.), *Language and masculinity* (pp. 47–64). London: Longman.

Christie, C. (2003). Politeness and the linguistic construction of gender in parliament: An analysis of transgressions and apology behaviour [online]. Sheffield Hallam Working Papers: Linguistic Politeness and Context. http://extra.shu.ac.uk/wpw/politeness/christie.htm. Accessed 27 Aug 2015.

Corner, J. (2000). Mediated persona and political culture: Dimensions of structure and process. *European Journal of Cultural Studies, 3*(3), 386–402.

Drake, P., & Higgins, M. (2012). Lights, Camera, Election: Celebrity, Performance and the 2010 UK General Election Leadership Debates. *The British Journal of Politics & International Relations,* 14 (3), 375–391.

Eckert, P. (1998). Gender and sociolinguistic variation. In J. Coates (Ed.), *Language and gender: A reader* (pp. 64–75). Oxford: Blackwell.

Edelsky, C., & Adams, K. (1990). Creating inequality: Breaking the rules in debates. *Journal of Language and Social Psychology, 9*(3), 171–190.

Fairclough, N. (1992). *Discourse and social change*. Cambridge: Polity Press.

Goffman, E. (1981). *Forms of talk*. Philadelphia: University of Pennsylvania Press.

Gumperz, J. (2001). Interactional sociolinguistics: A personal perspective. In D. Schiffrin, D. Tannen, & H. Hamilton (Eds.), *The handbook of discourse analysis* (pp. 213–228). Malden, MA: Wiley-Blackwell.

Hymes, D. H. (1972). Models of the interaction of language and social life. In J. Gumperz & D. Hymes (Eds.), *Directions in sociolinguistics: The ethnography* (pp. 35–71). Oxford: Blackwell.

Ilie, C. (2003). Discourse and metadiscourse in parliamentary debates. *Journal of Language and Politics, 2*(1), 71–92.

Ilie, C. (2013). Gendering confrontational rhetoric: Discursive disorder in the British and Swedish parliaments. *Democratization, 20*(3), 501–521.

Kavanagh, D., & Cowley, P. (2010). *The British general election of 2010.* Basingstoke: Palgrave Macmillan.

Lovenduski, J. (2014). Prime Minister's questions as political ritual at Westminster. In S. M. Rai & R. E. Johnson (Eds.), *Democracy in practice: Ceremony and ritual in parliament* (pp. 132–162). Basingstoke: Palgrave Macmillan.

Montgomery, M. (2001a). The uses of authenticity: 'Speaking from experience' in a UK election broadcast. *The Communication Review, 4*(4), 447–462.

Montgomery, M. (2001b). Defining 'authentic talk'. *Discourse Studies, 3*(4), 397–405.

Montgomery, M. (2010). Rituals of personal experience in television news interviews. *Discourse & Communication, 4*(2), 185–211.

Pomerantz, A., & Heritage, J. (2012). Preference. In J. Sidnell & T. Stivers (Eds.), *The handbook of conversation analysis* (pp. 210–228). Malden, MA: Wiley-Blackwell.

Sacks, H., Schegloff, E. A., & Jefferson, G. (1974). A simplest systematics for the organization of turn-taking for conversation. *Language, 50*(4), 696–735.

Shaw, S. (2000). Language, gender and floor apportionment in political debates. *Discourse & Society, 11*(3), 401–418.

Shaw, S. (2006). Governed by the rules? The female voice in Parliamentary debates. In J. Baxter (Ed.), *Speaking out: The female voice in public contexts* (pp. 81–102). Basingstoke: Palgrave Macmillan.

Shaw, S., *Women, language and politics.* Cambridge: Cambridge University Press (forthcoming).

Tannen, D. (1993). The relativity of linguistic strategies: Rethinking power and solidarity in gender and dominance. In D. Tannen (Ed.), *Gender and conversational interaction* (pp. 165–188). New York: Oxford University Press.

CHAPTER 3

Reception and Representation

Abstract This chapter examines the representation of the three female party leaders in a sample of election coverage taken from UK national newspapers. The analysis identifies a number of key themes in this coverage—noting that both gender and gendered styles of speaking were among press commentators' preoccupations—and discusses some of the rhetorical and linguistic devices that recurred in commentary on the women. While the personalized, trivializing, and stereotypical representations found by other researchers were a salient feature of the press discourse sampled, there was also a clear trend towards positive representations of women's performances in the debates, which can be related to the 'different voice' ideology of gender, language, and politics.

Keywords Election coverage • Female political leaders • Sexism • Tabloidization • UK press

Introduction

In contemporary western societies most political communication is mediated. Far more people watch TV debates, or read newspaper coverage of an election campaign, than meet political candidates face to face. The print, broadcast, and (increasingly) online media thus play a significant

© The Editor(s) (if applicable) and The Author(s) 2016
D. Cameron, S. Shaw, *Gender, Power and Political Speech*,
DOI 10.1057/978-1-137-58752-7_3

role in shaping the public perception of politicians. In this chapter we look at the way the media represented—and so contributed to shaping public perceptions of—the female politicians who figured prominently in GE2015.

It should be acknowledged, of course, that analysing media representations of the performances of politicians is not the same thing as analysing the reception of those performances by the public at large. People are not uncritical consumers of media representations, and their own judgements of events like the televised leaders' debates may differ from the judgements made by media commentators (in the concluding chapter we will briefly consider some other kinds of evidence [such as focus-group research] about the reception of politicians' debate performances by 'ordinary' viewers). However, we take it that the media are an influential source of the opinions and viewpoints with which people engage in the process of forming their own judgements: while media representations cannot be thought of as determining what individuals believe, they do play an important role in, as Cammaerts (2015) puts it, 'outlin[ing] the contours of public debate'. For our purposes, it is of particular interest to ask what media representations tell us about the contours of public discourse on gender and political leadership.

The media representation of female political leaders is a well-established topic in political communication research, and a number of studies have focused specifically on election coverage (Carlin and Winfrey 2009; Lawless 2009; Mäkelä et al. 2015; Meeks 2012, 2013; Semetko and Boomgaarden 2007). They have found that campaign coverage typically gives less attention to women than to men; that coverage of women shows a preoccupation with their appearance, clothing, personal relationships, and domestic roles; and that the media tend to judge female politicians by contradictory criteria, requiring them on the one hand to show they do not lack the 'masculine' qualities of authority and toughness, and on the other, to bring some distinctively 'feminine' quality to their roles.

Researchers at Loughborough University have made a comprehensive analysis of the media coverage of GE2015, and their quantitative findings reveal the usual pattern of female under-representation. Though women made up more than a quarter of Parliamentary candidates (Fawcett 2015), they comprised only just over 15 % of the politicians featured in campaign coverage (Harmer 2015a). Sixteen of the twenty individuals who featured most prominently in election coverage were men (Loughborough University Communication Research Centre 2015): the most prominent woman was Nicola Sturgeon, who ranked fourth, while the other three women in the top twenty were Natalie Bennett (12th), Samantha Cameron (15th), and Leanne Wood (17th). The list did not include any female politician who had served in Cabinet, in government, or indeed as an elected member of the Westminster Parliament. Only one of the women—Natalie Bennett—was even standing for election.

But while Loughborough's figures certainly show a gender imbalance, we would be cautious about interpreting them, on their own, as evidence of gender bias. Arguably what they reflect is the increasingly 'presidential' nature of British election coverage—its tendency to give most attention to party leaders, with a particular focus on those who are potential prime ministers. This had the effect of skewing the coverage towards men because most of the parties were led by men, including the two largest parties whose leaders were prime ministerial contenders. It was these two men, David Cameron and Ed Miliband, who topped Loughborough's list of the most prominently featured individuals, accounting between them for almost 30 % of all coverage of individual politicians. The third-ranked individual, Nick Clegg, had a score of 6.5 %, less than half of Cameron's or Miliband's. Nicola Sturgeon came just behind Clegg at 5.7 %, and just in front of Nigel Farage at 5.5 %.

The presence of Clegg, Sturgeon, and Farage in the top five reflects a specific feature of GE2015 coverage, the importance accorded to what has been dubbed the 'horse race' narrative (Cushion and Sambrook 2015), a story shaped by polls suggesting (wrongly, as it turned out) that the election would be a close contest in which no party would win an overall majority. This led the media to take more interest than usual in the smaller parties that might end up holding the balance of power. The amount of attention their leaders received reflected assumptions made during the campaign (albeit inaccurately in some cases) about where they would come in the race and what influence that would give them. Natalie Bennett and Leanne Wood appeared much further down the list than Clegg, Sturgeon, and Farage because their parties were expected to do much less well. But it was their status as party leaders in a multiparty 'horse race' that enabled these two women to break into the top twenty, ahead of many more established national figures, including the most senior Conservative and Labour women.

Arguably, then, the findings of quantitative analysis are compatible with the conclusion that male and female politicians received broadly comparable treatment. That is not to say they received equal coverage—clearly they did not—but their treatment was determined by the same criteria, that is, party leaders got far more coverage than 'ordinary' candidates, and the relative prominence given to leaders followed from the predicted position of their party in the electoral 'horse race'. The reasons why women received less attention than men were more directly related to these factors than to gender as such (a point demonstrated most clearly by the treatment of Nicola Sturgeon, who did get more attention than any male non-party leader). Of course, it is not a random coincidence that the main parties were led by men, but that says more about the parties' own gender bias than the media's.

However, there are important questions about the media representation of women which cannot be addressed in purely quantitative terms. While it is obviously relevant to ask whether women are equitably represented in terms of the quantity of coverage devoted to them, it is also necessary to consider the nature of that coverage: to ask not just *how much* is being said about women, but also *what* is being said, and what kind of language is being used to say it. These are the points we will concentrate on here. Rather than duplicate the quantitative work that has already done by others, we will use qualitative methods to analyse press discourse on GE2015—paying attention not only to its content, but also to its rhetorical construction and linguistic form. Two main questions, or sets of questions, will be addressed, the first looking generally at the discursive positioning of female politicians, while the second relates to our more specific interest in ideologies of gender and political speech:

(1) How did the media represent the most prominent female politicians in the campaign? To what extent (if any) were these women trivialized, sexualized, or otherwise stereotyped by gender, and what linguistic/rhetorical strategies were used to do this? Were similar strategies employed in presenting all of them, or were there individual differences?

(2) How did the media represent the female party leaders as public speakers (their skills, their styles, their voices, their effectiveness in the two TV debates), and how does this relate to the analysis of their performances which we presented in Chap. 2?

Some of the questions grouped under (1) have been touched on both in the Loughborough research already mentioned (e.g. Harmer 2015a), and in a collection of brief commentaries that appeared shortly after the election (Jackson and Thorsen 2015). One subject that has been debated is the media's tendency to trivialize female politicians by focusing on their appearance and their personal/domestic lives. This issue was raised by the UK feminist pressure group Fawcett, which mounted a campaign on social media using the hashtag #viewsnotshoes. Fawcett criticized not only the trivializing of female politicians, but also their under-representation in news coverage and the tendency for male politicians' wives to feature more prominently than women who were political actors in their own right (Fawcett 2015). However, other commentators noted that men were also represented in domestic settings and familial roles (both Cameron and Miliband made high-profile appearances in their kitchens), and that the prominence of their wives was a by-product of this portrayal of them as 'family men'. Karin Wahl-Jorgensen (2015: 24) suggested that 'politicians are now not only required to show themselves as decisive leaders, but also loving fathers and husbands who contribute to domestic work, including cooking and child care'. Emily Harmer (2015b), by contrast, saw the 'family man' discourse as a version of the traditional patriarchal narrative that portrays men as strong leaders, protecting the country in the same way they protect their wives and children—a model of leadership which is not readily available to women, whether or not they have families (Lewis 2015).

There has also been debate on the prevalence and meaning of overt sexism in the reporting of GE2015. While some commentators (e.g. Savigny 2015) argue that sexism was as much of a problem in this campaign as in past ones, others (e.g. Ross 2015) believe that there has been a shift in attitudes. One of the points at issue here is how to interpret the attacks made on Nicola Sturgeon by the right-wing press. Ross acknowledges the misogyny of some representations of Sturgeon, but also wants to recognize that this hostility reflected her opponents' assessment of her as an able politician, and as such a genuine threat.

These points will be explored further in our own analysis of election coverage drawn from the UK press. Given that we do not have space to analyse the full range of media output (print, broadcast, and online), there are two main reasons why we have chosen to concentrate on newspapers. One is the extent to which they set agendas for the media more generally. Although research suggests that most UK voters get most of their information from broadcast news and current affairs programmes, the broadcasters themselves are significantly influenced by newspaper reporting and commentary (Beckett 2015). In GE2015 there was also considerable interest in the role of online social media, but how to interpret the data and assess their significance remains a matter of debate (Margetts and Hale 2015), with some researchers suggesting that their impact on public opinion was in fact very limited compared with that of the more traditional media (Cammaerts 2015). The second reason for focusing on the press is that the kind and range of ideological discourses we are interested in are more likely to be found in newspapers, which are not subject to the political impartiality rules that govern broadcasting in the UK (and are particularly stringent in the case of election coverage).

SAMPLE

Our analysis is based on a sample of newspaper articles retrieved using the database Lexis UK. The parameters of the search were set to retrieve all items which (a) appeared in a UK newspaper, (b) were published between 31 March (the day after Parliament was dissolved) and 7 May (the day of the election), and (c) mentioned any of the three female party leaders by name in any part of the text. This procedure returned 373 items, which were then read closely to exclude duplicates and pieces which were not concerned with GE2015. (For instance, Sturgeon was mentioned in passing in a report about Hillary Clinton's announcement that she planned to run for President in the USA.) The sample was further filtered to exclude items from press agencies, local newspapers, and the Scottish, Welsh, or Northern Irish editions of national titles. These items were retained and may be referred to where relevant, but the main focus of our analysis will be the coverage which appeared in either national (i.e. all-UK) or English editions of newspapers—219 items in all. We chose to restrict our scope in this way partly for reasons of space, but also because of the complications that would have been introduced by using an aggregated sample. Two of the women leaders represented parties which were only contesting seats in Scotland or Wales; both the quantity of coverage they received and the editorial stance taken towards their parties differed significantly in their home territories and in the rest of the UK. (For instance, one major title, the *Sun*, supported the SNP in Scotland while opposing it vigorously in its English edition.) Our primary interest was in the reception of female politicians as important players on the national political stage, and therefore we chose to concentrate on the national/English press.

Our sample includes material from both the major London-based national daily newspapers—the *Times, Telegraph, Independent* and its 'concise' stable-mate the *i, Guardian, Express, Mail, Mirror, Sun* and *Star*—and the associated Sunday titles (the *Observer, Sunday Express, Sunday Times, Sunday Telegraph, Independent on Sunday, Mail on Sunday*, and so on). Editorially, the majority of these titles supported the Conservatives (with the *Express* also showing some sympathy for UKIP, to which its proprietor was a major donor). The *Independent* came out in favour of a renewed Conservative/Liberal Democrat coalition, while its Sunday sister-paper declined to endorse any party. The *Guardian*, its Sunday sister-title the *Observer*, and the *Mirror* supported Labour. Since we wanted to investigate the range of representations and perceptions encountered by readers of a newspaper's election coverage, the items sampled were not limited to news reports, but also included features of various kinds, regular columns, one-off opinion pieces, and editorials. Nor was the sample limited to items dealing only with the three female party leaders. We searched for items in which any one of the women was mentioned by name in any part of the text, and this returned a mixture of items focusing on a single individual (the largest number of items in this category focused on Nicola Sturgeon), items discussing the women as a group—sometimes alongside other female politicians—and items discussing both the male and the female leaders. This last category was the largest overall: though it cannot provide a basis for a full account of the way the men were represented in election coverage, it does enable us to compare the representation of the male and female party leaders in articles dealing with both. Many of these articles are reports on or assessments of the male and female leaders' performance in the two televised debates, and as such, they are of particular interest for the purposes of this book.

THEMES

A number of themes emerged from qualitative analysis of our sample. We will begin by summarizing them briefly and then proceed to a more detailed examination of each one:

(1) There were differences as well as similarities in the representation of the three female party leaders as individuals. Differences were apparent in the amount of coverage individual leaders received; in the balance between positive, negative, and 'neutral' coverage; and in the particular qualities that were highlighted in representations of each woman.

(2) Commentary on appearance, clothing, perceived sexual attractiveness, and personal and family relationships was a salient aspect of the coverage of the female party leaders. However, men were by no means immune from this tendency.

(3) Gender was a theme in its own right: notwithstanding the individual differences mentioned above, the three female party leaders were often referred to collectively as 'the women' and discussed in terms that foregrounded their shared gender (and alleged difference from men) rather than their shared political commitments.

(4) Women's speech styles and public speaking abilities were also a theme, often linked to the broader discourse on gender mentioned in (3).

The Women as Individuals: Similarities and Differences

All three women leaders received both positive and negative coverage, as well as 'neutral' coverage (straightforward factual reporting of their words and actions during the campaign). However, the balance was different for each individual woman, and the differences reflected newspapers' political allegiances as well as writers' personal judgements.

None of the female leaders benefited from the editorial support of any London-based newspaper. Most of the press supported the Conservatives, and was hostile both to the leftist politics espoused by the female-led parties and to the nationalism espoused by two of them. Among the minority of non-Conservative newspapers, a couple declined to support any party, but most supported Labour, which was in direct competition with the SNP in Scotland, Plaid Cymru in Wales, and the Greens across the country. A newspaper's attitude to the women leaders and their parties therefore tended to reflect a mixture of its general ideological sympathies (e.g. left-leaning titles with middle-class readerships tended to be more positive about the Greens than others), political calculations about what kind of threat they represented to the party the newspaper did support (this particularly affected attitudes to Nicola Sturgeon, since the SNP's strength in Scotland had the potential to thwart both Labour and Conservative ambitions), and perceptions of a leader's performance in the campaign.

Before the first TV debate, coverage of the three women was dominated by items profiling them for an audience which was assumed to know little or nothing about them. These items appeared under titles such as 'Who is Natalie Bennett?' (*Mirror*, 1 April), 'Who is Leanne Wood, who are Plaid Cymru and what do they stand for?' (*Independent*, 2 April), and 'Do you really know who these women are?' (*Telegraph*, 2 April). After the debate, the focus shifted from 'who are they?' to 'how did they do?' Though a number of these post-debate commentaries focused on 'the women' as a single entity—a theme we consider in more detail below—this was also the point at which the three leaders started to become individually differentiated.

Most coverage of Natalie Bennett was critical: her campaign was punctuated by a series of events that prompted negative evaluations of her competence, intelligence, and political judgement. Bennett gave two radio interviews (one on a London station just prior to the sampling period and one on the BBC's *Today* programme in the second week of it) in which she was deemed to have performed poorly ('Natalie Bennett's excruciating slip-ups', *Telegraph*, 10 April; 'Nat's the fluff of legend', *Sun*, 9 April). Later in the campaign there was controversy about views her partner had expressed in a blog a few years earlier ('50 shades of Green', *Mirror*, 19 April; 'Green leader's partner blogs on rape fantasies', *Mail*, 20 April) and in the final week, further controversy about a suggestion that the Green party would be open to legalizing marriages involving three people ('A ménage à trois in sandals is unthinkable', *Telegraph*, 5 May). While some articles focused on key policy issues (e.g. the party's commitment to scrapping Trident, Britain's nuclear deterrent), these concerns were less prominent than commentary on Bennett's 'gaffes' and, in the right-wing press, on the extreme and bizarre views she and her party were said to espouse.

Leanne Wood was the least well-known of the party leaders before the campaign, and one poll found that after several weeks of campaigning, she still prompted the 'most neutral' response from voters ('Chart reveals which party leaders we like', *Independent*, 2 May). The national press took a similar view: Wood received less attention than the other female party leaders, and most of the coverage she did get was neither strongly positive nor strongly negative (with one important exception: her most salient intervention in the first TV debate, taking issue with Nigel Farage's assertion that immigrants with HIV were exploiting the health service, was generally positively received). Her record of opposition to the monarchy (she was once excluded from the Welsh Assembly's debating chamber for referring to the Queen as 'Mrs Windsor') was occasionally used by right-wing newspapers to present her as an extremist (e.g. 'Risk to Queen', *Sun*, 3 May). But despite making no attempt to downplay her socialism ('My politics are to the left of Labour', *Independent*, 16 April), Wood did not attract the same hostility as her ally Nicola Sturgeon: negative coverage tended to be patronizing rather than hostile. The difference probably reflects the 'political calculation' factor: Plaid Cymru in Wales was less strong than the SNP in Scotland, and was therefore regarded as peripheral to the outcome of the election.

Nicola Sturgeon was the most extensively covered of the three women, and commentary on her encompassed a spectrum of views from extremely positive to extremely negative. In fact, many items in our sample were both at once: they evaluated Sturgeon's campaign performance positively (her competence as a leader and her debating skills were acknowledged by commentators of all political persuasions) while expressing negative views of her personal and political motivations (a dual stance epitomized by headlines like the *Telegraph*'s 'She'll charm you—but don't fall for the siren of the SNP' (2 April)). This was the main position adopted not only by the right-wing press, which feared a Labour–SNP alliance, but also by the Labour-supporting *Mirror*, which feared (not wrongly, as it turned out) that the swing from Labour to SNP in Scotland, along with English voters' resistance to a Scottish anti-unionist party wielding significant influence over the UK government, would produce a Conservative victory ('Nicola Sturgeon's TV win could leave David Cameron in charge by default', *Mirror*, 2 April). The only title that largely avoided this kind of commentary was the *Guardian*.

In relation to Sturgeon, the main theme of the commentary that appeared after the first TV debate was how impressively she had performed ('Sturgeon star of the show', *Sun*, 3 April), and how well her performance had been received by the viewing public ('Can I vote for the SNP, voters ask', *Independent*, 3 April). Similarly positive reports on her performance and popularity continued to appear throughout the campaign ('The SNP are climbing high and Nicola Sturgeon is the new rock and roll', *Times*, 21 April; 'The rise and rise of surging Sturgeon', *Mail*, 27 April), but from 4 April onwards, when James Chapman's *Mail* article 'Is this the most dangerous woman in Britain?' appeared, there was also a steady increase in negative coverage. On 5 April the *Sunday Express* produced the first of a number of items in our sample ('The truth behind SNP "cult" leader Nicola Sturgeon'), portraying Sturgeon as ambitious, driven, controlling, and autocratic. This representation was not confined to the right-wing press: a week later, in the *Mirror*, former Labour deputy Prime Minister John Prescott compared Sturgeon to Margaret Thatcher ('Irn-Bru lady's not for trusting', *Mirror*, 12 April). As the campaign progressed, the idea of Sturgeon as a puppet master with Ed Miliband as her puppet, introduced by the Conservative Party in its campaign advertising, began to feature prominently in the press ('Puppet master Nicola', *Mail on Sunday*, 19 April). Senior Conservative politicians reinforced this message: Ann Widdecombe proclaimed in the *Express* (22 April) that '[t]here is only one way to prevent Britain being ruled by Nicola Sturgeon', while the *Sunday*

Telegraph ran an interview with the Conservative Home Secretary Theresa May headed 'Don't let Nicola Sturgeon call the shots' (3 May). Some of the negative coverage Sturgeon received was overtly (and on occasion, grotesquely) sexist. References to her childlessness formed one element in the recurring attacks on her as an overambitious political obsessive; this, together with the personal insults and sexualized images that appeared in some newspapers, prompted a number of articles deploring the sexism of election press reporting. Sturgeon's own complaints on this score were also widely reported ('Sturgeon attacks sexist questions', *Mail*, 23 April). Some of the most hostile pieces were written by women: the *Telegraph* columnist Allison Pearson contributed two strongly worded pieces attacking Sturgeon ('It's time to say "Bye Bye, Baby"' on 22 April and 'I know how to solve a problem like Nicola Sturgeon—release the lynx' on 29 April), while Amanda Platell wrote a piece in the *Mail* headed 'Why we women can't stand Sturgeon' (18 April). But while complaints of sexism in the press coverage of Sturgeon were undoubtedly justified, we are inclined to agree with Karen Ross (2015) that this was not just the everyday, reflex contempt for women which remains common in parts of the British press. Rather, Nicola Sturgeon was attacked—in ways the other two female party leaders were not—because she was assessed as a credible political threat. The fact that she was a woman meant that sexism could be deployed as a weapon in the campaign against her, but that campaign was not motivated primarily or mainly by her gender (in that respect, arguably, she does have something in common with Margaret Thatcher). That is not, of course, to deny that sexism can be a powerful weapon which puts female politicians at a collective disadvantage (we explore this point further in the next section). It is only to acknowledge that in Nicola Sturgeon's case, it was more a means to an end than an end in itself.

Views and Shoes: The Personalization of Politics

Media scholars (e.g. Esser 1999; McLachlan and Golding 2000) have drawn attention to the phenomenon of 'tabloidization' in the British press, meaning (among other things) an increase in the proportion of 'soft' content designed to entertain readers (and sell newspapers) by focusing on opinions, personalities, and 'human interest' stories rather than facts, issues, and investigative reporting or in-depth analysis. Election coverage does not stand apart from this trend. A substantial proportion of the items in our sample appeared outside the traditional locations for political reporting and comment (e.g. the main domestic news section and the editorial/op-ed pages), and followed the conventions of genres such as the profile, interview, lifestyle feature, fashion feature, quiz, or personal opinion piece. In addition, there were items which, though generically news reports, took a deliberately 'light', humorous, or quirky approach (e.g. a story headed 'Was it grey, green or ice-blue?' [*Mail*, 17 April], about the colour of a dress worn by Nicola Sturgeon).

Since our sample was constructed by looking for mentions of the female party leaders, it is not surprising that we found more material of this kind relating to women than to men, especially in the fashion and lifestyle categories. Numerous pieces were written about the female party leaders' wardrobes and hairstyles, and in Nicola Sturgeon's case, the more radical image makeover she was said to have undergone. Fashion writers exploited the visibility the TV debates gave to women to put a topical spin on such well-worn subjects as the power of the red dress or the return of the colour pink. However, what did surprise us, especially given that we were not specifically looking for it, was the relatively large number of items in our sample which did discuss men in the ways deplored by Fawcett's 'views not shoes' campaign. Even the preoccupation with shoes themselves was not exclusively a concern about female footwear: much was made of the revelation that Ed Miliband had sent campaign staff out to buy shoes before the first debate ('ITV Leaders Debate: Ed Miliband banks on 'sensible' new shoes from Clarks to kick rivals into touch', *Mirror*, 2 April).

Most coverage of this variety was essentially apolitical, but some of it was more clearly linked to the central political contest, with descriptions of the women leaders' physical appearance used in conjunction with, or as proxies for, attacks on their competence or their political views. The most frequent target of these attacks was Nicola Sturgeon. In the *Telegraph*, a commentator on the first debate described her as 'brisk, strict, with little sharp rodent eyes and a hairdo the shape of a Tunnock's Tea Cake' ('Shout, shout, interruption, shout', 3 April), while the same paper's Allison Pearson said that her haircut 'made her look like the missing, sixth Bay City Roller' ('It's time to say "Bye Bye, Baby"', 22 April). Sturgeon was also compared to one of the Krankies (a Scottish comedy double-act) and described by the serial controversialist Katie Hopkins as 'a short poison ginger dwarf'. Criticisms of Natalie Bennett focused more on her intellect, judgement, and speaking skills, but her appearance and clothing drew some negative comments, with the *Mail* describing her as '[Australian cricket commentator] Richie Benaud in drag' (April 3). Leanne Wood, by contrast, was portrayed as a political lightweight through references to her youthful appearance and feminine self-presentation ('she looked like a

16-year-old whose date had failed to show up for the prom' was the verdict of a commentator in the *Telegraph* after the first debate). A similar effect was produced by references to her 'sexy' Welsh-accented voice; the TV personality Richard Madeley commented, for instance (*Express*, April 11): 'I can't get enough of Plaid Cymru leader Leanne Wood. That gorgeous accent! I could listen to it all day. It's warmer than sunlight shining through a jar of honey'—an assessment which did not suggest a primary concern with the political content of Wood's discourse.

Our sample also contained items in which comparable personal remarks were made about men. Some of these were also 'fluff', like a piece posing the question: 'Has Michael Gove had botox?' (*Mirror*, 15 April). But in other cases, comments on a male politician's physical appearance were used to make negative judgements on his credentials as a leader. This was true, for instance, of the comments made by many commentators about the fact that Nigel Farage had been visibly sweating during the first TV debate. It was also a feature of commentary on the social media 'Milifandom' trend portraying Ed Miliband as a sex symbol. This prompted such responses as an *Express* article headed 'The ugly truth about Ed Miliband' (26 April), which began: 'A girlfriend of mine used to have a thing for Kim Jong-il'. The (female) writer is not much kinder to Miliband's main competitor: 'Resembling the love child of one of the Moomins and Data from *Star Trek*, David Cameron is hardly model material either, but his looks certainly aren't as "unfortunate" as his Labour rival's'. She explicitly notes that 'facial fascism' now affects politicians of both sexes: if looks mattered less, the Conservative Party might still be led by the clever but odd-looking William Hague. That argument might seem unconvincing, though, in the light of the prominence given to another odd-looking man who is widely tipped as a future Conservative leader, Boris Johnson. The *Express* (23 April) reported that Johnson was the politician most voters wanted to have sex with, though his looks were 'unfortunate' enough to prompt one (male) commentator to describe him as 'a fat, buffoonish yellow-haired spectre' (*Mirror*, 7 May).

The press took an interest in the spouses and partners of both male and female leaders ('Meet him and her indoors', *Express*, 20 April; 'Leaders outshone by their better halves', *Telegraph*, 23 April). However, the male leaders appeared to encourage this (and their wives appeared to go along with it) to a greater extent than the female leaders, who did not generally emulate Cameron, Clegg, and Miliband in making high-profile campaign appearances with their partners. (Sturgeon's husband was involved in the campaign because he also held a senior position in the SNP, but Leanne Wood insisted on privacy for her partner; Natalie Bennett was obliged to point out that her partner was not a Green Party member when views he had expressed in his blog were reported in a bid to embarrass her.)

All this suggests that it is not entirely accurate to say that the media focused on male politicians' views and female politicians' shoes (or their sexual attractiveness or their domestic lives). But that is not to say there is no gender bias here, or that the problem is a simple matter of women receiving a greater quantity of trivializing coverage than men. The problem is rather that men and women are differently positioned in relation to this kind of commentary, and its effects are therefore not the same in each case. A preoccupation with women's appearance and sexual attractiveness reinforces a pre-existing gender inequality (the tendency to judge women more by their looks than their actions or words) in a way that the same preoccupation, applied to men, does not. It also mobilizes assumptions about the relationship of gender to power and authority which pose particular problems for women in leadership positions.

For men, power and authority are seen as natural and desirable: what male politicians are most likely to be criticized for is a perceived lack of authority, which may also be figured as a lack of masculinity. The representation of Ed Miliband in the Conservative press exemplifies this. First, he was disparaged for his failure to match the alpha-male ideal, then he was ridiculed when his supporters attempted to counter that criticism by casting him as a sex symbol. For women, by contrast, power and authority are seen as unnatural, undesirable, and de-sexing. This view is reflected in the 'humorous' comments quoted above, which either describe the female leaders as parodic versions of men (Jimmy Krankie, the sixth Bay City Roller, Richie Benaud in drag) or else present them in terms which reference a common stereotype of women in authority as either sexless or sexually repulsive (e.g. 'brisk, strict, with little sharp rodent eyes'). This kind of stereotyping occurs frequently in our sample, and we will examine it in more detail later on when we turn to some of the rhetorical and linguistic features of GE2015 press coverage.

'THE WOMEN' VERSUS 'THE MEN': GENDER AS A THEME

The question of women's role in politics is addressed by 23 of the 219 items in our sample, making it a salient theme overall. A small number of items are either news reports on events such as the launch of Labour's Women's Manifesto ('Launched from a sandpit', *Telegraph*, 16 April) or profiles of women other than the party leaders ('Women MPs to look out for after the election', *Telegraph*, 29 April). Most, however, are opinion pieces in which the visibility of the three female leaders prompts an assessment of women's political contribution, whether positive (Edwina Currie hailed a 'women's revolution' in the *Telegraph* [3 April]) or from a perspective that emphasizes their continuing under-representation in positions of power ('Why women need a stronger voice in politics', *Observer*, 5 April; 'We should be arguing for more women in power', *Independent*, 6 April).

Many of these pieces raise the subject of women's contribution in the context of commenting on the two TV debates. In this subset of coverage, there is a recurrent tendency for writers to construct a rhetorical opposition between 'the women' and 'the men', in which 'the women' are clearly marked as the positive term. After the first debate, for instance, headlines included 'Nigel Farage lost the debate and the women were the winners' (*Mirror*, 2 April); 'Leaders debate: it was the women wot won it' (*Guardian*, 3 April); 'The women took on Nigel while the men blamed each other' (*Times*, 3 April); and 'Gentlemen, you are the weakest link' (*Sunday Times*, 5 April). This theme also appeared in coverage of the Scottish contest, which pitted Nicola Sturgeon against, among others, the Scottish Conservative leader Ruth Davidson ('The women are the winners', *Observer*, 3 May), and it resurfaced in retrospective summaries at the end of the campaign. On polling day the *Mirror* opined that 'women were the best performers' ('It's been a kitchen nightmare', 7 May); the next day a *Telegraph* article suggested that women's 'thoughtful, measured contributions' to the TV debates had 'brought a certain dignity to an occasion which could have descended into chaos and rancour' ('How women took centre stage in a man's world', 8 May). It is notable that these positive assessments of 'the women' were often made by commentators who had no time for their actual political views, writing in newspapers which harped relentlessly on the dire consequences that would follow if Sturgeon emerged as a literal 'winner'. If not political ideology, though, what was this 'women versus men' discourse about?

A similar discourse on gender has been identified in other contexts. In Finland, for example, Mäkelä et al. (2015) have analysed the press's treatment of Jutta Urpilainen, a candidate for the leadership of the Social Democratic Party in 2008, finding that her femaleness was often presented as an asset in and of itself: at a time when her party was felt to be in need of modernization, the idea of a woman leader, someone outside the traditionally male political establishment, symbolized a commitment to a new and different kind of politics. In the very different context of the US Republican Party, it has been argued that the same symbolic equation of femaleness with outsider status was one element (though not the only one) in the meteoric rise of Sarah Palin (Davies 2015; Meeks 2013). And in GE2015 coverage there is evidence of a similar symbolism. Discourse on 'the women' portrayed them as a fresh, modern alternative by virtue of their status as outsiders to the 'Westminster boys' club'.

Comments contrasting women's fresh approach to the stale formulas of the male establishment appeared in newspapers representing a range of party allegiances. In the Conservative *Times* ('Leaders' wives should get out of the kitchen', 11 May), Janice Turner remarked that '[t]he only upside to this election so far was hearing three women leaders speak at the seven-way debate rather than the eternal line-up of identikit men', while A.A. Gill, commenting on the same event in the *Sunday Times* ('Gentlemen, you are the weakest link', 5 April), said that the women's performances had 'highlighted how brutally formulaic the men were in their panto melodrama'. Even the ultra-traditionalist *Telegraph* thought the positive reception given to the women in the two debates showed that 'Britain is ready for a new kind of politics' ('The leaders' debate hug', 17 April). Meanwhile, at the other end of the political spectrum, the Labour-supporting *Guardian*'s Michael Billington wrote that 'if anyone emerged with credit from the TV marathon, it was the female partici-pants who actually responded to what they were hearing and who seemed to be living in the moment' ('It was the women wot won it', 3 May). Yasmin Alibhai-Brown, writing in the *Independent* (which was backing a second Conservative–Liberal Democrat coalition), suggested that 'female audacity and imagination have made the male leaders - all of them - look cowardly and deeply unimaginative… Sturgeon, Wood and Bennett have proved politicians are not all the same' ('Finally, political sisters are doin it for us', 20 April).

There was surprisingly little dissent from this view, but one commenta-tor, Melanie McDonagh, did express impatience with a rhetoric she found both condescending and politically partisan ('Women don't have to be touchy-feely to be political', *Independent*, 17 April):

> There are two ways of looking at the challengers' debate last week in respect of women in politics. One, the near-universal view is, aah, how lovely to see three "feisty", articulate women take on the male establishment… The other view, mine, is that it was a deeply dispiriting 90 minutes, which seemed to

suggest that women conform to a single political stereotype, viz, the left-of-centre, tax-and-spend kind.

Our analysis supports McDonagh's contention that the rhetorical opposition between the women and 'the male establishment' often traded on patronizing and stereotypical views of gender difference. Michael Billington, for instance, commented in his *Guardian* piece that 'it was cheering to hear the SNP's Nicola Sturgeon, who seems more full of sass and bite every time I hear her, interrupting a piece of Clegg-waffle with cries of "Rubbish"'. The *Mirror* noted that 'the three women leaders... sang their songs beautifully' ('Nigel Farage lost leaders' debate and the women were the winners', 2 April). This language might seem to warrant McDonagh's implicit comparison with adults watching fondly as children or pets perform ('aah, how lovely'). Another 'positive' stereotype that arguably does female politicians no favours was wheeled out by Richard Madeley, who suggested in the *Express* ('The best PMs we never had', 2 May) that 'sadly top quality ladies are not often attracted to the dirty, nasty old political game. They are not greedy or vicious enough and know there's more to life than climbing a greasy pole'. This piece argued (and was not the only one to do so) that the male party leaders' wives might have made better leaders than their husbands, had they not, as women, had more important things to do with their lives.

In their discussion of the Finnish case, Mäkelä et al. (2015) point out that the 'women are refreshingly different' discourse typically coexists with others which are in tension with it. Femaleness may be figured as both a positive quality (women bring something fresh and different to political leadership) and a negative one (women lack the authority and toughness leadership requires). Women are thus required, in effect, to achieve the impossible feat of being both different from men and the same as men. Individual women who display authority and toughness may also come under fire for being too much like men.

This last accusation was a thread running through almost all negative commentary on Nicola Sturgeon, who was vilified for such offences as being ambitious, having no children, and letting her husband do most of the cooking. By late April the criticism had become so relentless that Sturgeon herself spoke out on the subject, while newspapers not involved in it produced a series of articles documenting and deploring the media's sexism. Much of this meta-commentary appeared in the *Guardian*. Roy Greenslade contributed a piece headed 'Nicola Sturgeon emerges as Tory press election demon' (21 April); the next day Jessica Elgot collated the 'Worst Nicola Sturgeon insults', while Peter Bradshaw objected at length to one particular insult, the comparison of Sturgeon with the character of Wee Jimmy Krankie ('Not nice, not funny', 22 April). Having conceded that high-profile politicians of both sexes must expect to receive a certain amount of personal abuse, Bradshaw went on to argue:

> The Krankie joke is different. It's consciously punching down, smacking down a perceived upstart, someone who's above herself. And the nasty little point about the Wee Jimmy Krankie crack is that this is a female absurdly pretending to be male - and there are plenty of people of every political stripe in the boys' club made uneasy by Sturgeon.

The coverage that prompted most criticism came from the *Sun*, which produced an image (inspired by a music video featuring Miley Cyrus) that showed Sturgeon astride a wrecking ball dressed in a tartan crop top and knickers. A *Sun* piece headed 'Sisterhood politics won't be ladylike' was accompanied by a cartoon in which the three female party leaders (dubbed 'the scarlet sisterhood') were, in Jessica Elgot's words, 'mocked up as buxom Bond girls with visible nipples through sheer red dresses and crowding around a sweating Ed Miliband' ('Worst Nicola Sturgeon insults', *Guardian*, 22 April). This use of sexualized imagery is another media tactic that positions women and men differently (or rather, takes advantage of the social fact that they are already positioned differently with respect to sexual objectification). Whereas the images associated with 'Milifandom' were not intended to demean their object (even if they were used by his opponents to ridicule him), the *Sun*'s intention was to put Sturgeon and the other women in their (subordinate) place.

The fact that sexism became an issue rather than passing unchallenged gives some support to Ross's argument (Ross 2015) that there has been a shift in public attitudes. However, it could be argued that this shift has been quite limited. The media critique of sexism was largely a matter of upmarket newspapers criticizing the crude tactics of the 'red top' tabloids—a gesture which would have no effect on the tabloid writers and their readers, and which allowed titles like the *Guardian* to present themselves as critics of sexism while saying nothing about the less obvious examples that appeared in their own pages (would Michael Billington have described a male politician as 'full of sass and bite'?)

Women as Public Speakers

Since a great deal of commentary on all the party leaders focused on their performance in the two national TV debates, it is not surprising to find that the linguistic behaviour of politicians was frequently a topic of discussion. In comments on the leaders' styles of speaking, we find evidence both of the gendered language ideologies which are one subject of this book and of the way those ideologies inflect the judgements made on women speakers.

Commentary on the debates contains numerous references to what we have called the 'different voice' ideology of gender and political speech. A striking example appeared in the *Yorkshire Post* on the day after the election under the headline 'Nicola Sturgeon has inspired women and given hope' (both the source and the date place it outside our sample, but we quote it here as a particularly clear illustration of the point under discussion). It begins with this vignette:

> It was around 1 am on polling night when I finally switched off the TV, disappointed and irritated that yet again, two men were arguing, loudly, irascibly. I can't recall who they were now...

The writer goes on to argue that the leaders' debates had given the public a glimpse of a different way of doing politics:

> There were three women...not just holding their own, but setting new standards, openly supportive of each other, straightforward, fair, no bullying, no posturing. Frankly, they made the men look uniformly grey, out of date, superficial, even trivial.

This text makes use of the rhetorical opposition discussed above between 'the women' and 'the men', but it focuses on verbal behaviour as a symbol of the difference, contrasting men's arguing and shouting with women's supportiveness, men's bullying with women's fairness, and men's posturing with women's straightforwardness. The image of interchangeable men shouting was one that had recurred during the campaign, both in media commentary and in the utterances of politicians. Labour's Deputy Leader Harriet Harman was quoted as saying, 'Too often, women feel politics is just a group of men shouting at each other' ('At last, political sisters are doin it for us', *Independent*, 20 April). Natalie Bennett told an interviewer that she wanted to change the culture of Westminster, moving away from 'the image of MPs making noises at each other across the chamber in Prime Minister's Questions' ('What the women party leaders really want', *Telegraph*, 27 April).

The *Times*'s Ann Treneman expressed a more sceptical view of women's 'different voice'. She noted that before the first debate, there had been 'speculation about whether the fact that three of the leaders were women would change the tone of the debate and make it less aggressive, less shouty', but went on to observe that in the event, the women had not shied away from argument and conflict. It was Wood and Sturgeon who took issue with Nigel Farage's comments on immigrants (in Wood's case, by issuing a stern rebuke) while 'the men just stood there...looking earnest' ('The women took on Nigel while the men blamed each other', *Times*, 3 April). Yet the 'different voice' stereotype continued to be referenced throughout the campaign.

At the same time, individual assessments of the women's performance in the debates suggested a preference for adversarial speech. Positive comments on Nicola Sturgeon (of which, as we have noted already, there were many) expressed that preference clearly, repeatedly using combat metaphors in descriptions of her verbal tactics. After the first debate, for instance, the *Mirror*'s Kevin Maguire contrasted Sturgeon favourably with Farage, remarking that 'she landed punches. He punched himself in the face' (2 April). After the second debate, Mikey Smith praised Sturgeon's 'brilliant slap down of Ukip leader Nigel Farage for blaming everything on immigration. When he butted in saying the debate was "just astonishing", she hit back to cheers: "Yes you are"' ('Nicola Sturgeon verdict', *Mirror*, 16 April). A sketch writer in the *Telegraph* (20 April) commented that 'Labour supporters in England must yearn to have a sword-swinging gladiator like Ms Sturgeon as their leader'.

But adversarial strategies were only treated as praiseworthy when used with the skill Sturgeon displayed. Used by a less gifted female speaker, they prompted a different response. As we noted in Chap. 2, there was a point during the second debate when the floor was being monopolised by Ed Miliband and Nigel Farage, and a frustrated Natalie Bennett tried to cut in by raising her voice and asserting that it was her turn. The *Mirror* (16 April) reported this under the heading 'Angry Natalie Bennett loses her temper with Ed Miliband as BBC debate descends into shouting match; the Greens show their claws as emotions run high over the NHS'. The report continues: 'Natalie Bennett dramatically lost her temper with Ed Miliband tonight when she was forced to shout over him and Nigel Farage during the BBC election debate'. In our analysis of the relevant sequence, we pointed out that Bennett's intervention was extreme: no other participant attempted to gain the floor by shouting as loudly as this. Nevertheless, the way the *Mirror* reported it suggests a gendered double standard. Bennett's deviance from the accepted norms is not criticized in the way the *Yorkshire Post* writer criticizes the men arguing loudly on TV, as boorish and tiresome; rather she is figured as over-emotional and out of control, losing her temper and 'showing her claws'. It might also be observed that Nigel Farage's behaviour during the same sequence could also have been described as 'dramatically losing his temper': Farage not only raised his voice, he also called an opponent a liar. This was also extreme behaviour, but the *Mirror* apparently considered it less noteworthy.

Not using adversarial strategies could also be held against a female speaker. Though in the abstract women's more consensual style was cited with approval, concrete examples of consensual discourse moves were not usually evaluated positively. Leanne Wood, for instance, was criticised for 'failing to really get stuck in at key moments in the [second] debate. "I agree with quite a lot of what was said there", she said meekly at one point during the debate on defence' ('Leanne Wood verdict', *Mirror*, 17 April). Agreeing with other contributors rather than arguing with them—an example of the cooperative and supportive approach associated with women's 'different voice'—is recoded here as 'meek', and thus as a failure on Wood's part to meet the standards political speech is judged by.

The coexistence of conflicting ideologies of gender and political speech (one proposing that women are and should be different from men, the other proposing that their effectiveness as politicians depends on being able to 'land punches' in competition with men) is a problem for women in positions of political leadership. It sets up contradictory expectations which women can fail to meet if they are perceived as either too far from the male norm (like the 'meek' Leanne Wood) or too close to it, given that they are not actually male (like the 'angry' Natalie Bennett). One (approving) description of Nicola Sturgeon as 'combative without seeming aggressive' gives some indication of how hard it is to get the balance exactly right: the line between 'combative' and 'aggressive' behaviour is as fine as the semantic distinction between the words themselves.

So far this chapter has identified some major themes and rhetorical structures in press coverage of the female party leaders, and has related these to wider discourses on gender, language, and politics (e.g. the 'different voice' discourse). But there are also some patterns in our sample which cut across the thematic categories. In the final part of the chapter, we look at some of the rhetorical and linguistic choices which communicated messages about gender in a less direct way.

FIGURING FEMALE POLITICIANS: ARCHETYPES AND METAPHORS

Earlier we noted that the powerful woman is an anomalous figure: whereas power and masculinity are congruent with one another, power and femininity are not. In her classic text *Men and Women of the Corporation* (1993—the first edition appeared in 1977), the management theorist Rosabeth Kanter proposed that one way in which female authority is made culturally intelligible is through a set of categories based on historically established archetypes of female power. The four main archetypes Kanter identified were the 'Mother' (whose authority is associated with nurturance and self-sacrifice), the 'Seductress' (who uses her sexuality to gain influence over men), the 'Pet' (whose unthreatening femininity appeals to men's desire to protect her) and the 'Iron Maiden' (who exercises power directly, and is often regarded as 'masculine' and intimidating). Kanter refers to these as 'role traps': while on the one hand they help to legitimate the exercise of power by a woman, on the other, they restrict her scope for action and ensure that her behaviour will be interpreted in terms of her gender rather than her individual qualities.

In a recent reframing of Kanter's work, the discourse analyst Judith Baxter (2012) argues that Kanter's archetypes should not be seen as fixed roles in which individuals are eternally 'trapped', but rather as discursive resources which women themselves can exploit, shifting between positions to achieve particular goals in particular contexts. In her work on senior women in British FTSE (Financial Times Stock Exchange) companies, Baxter shows how women deploy these resources to position themselves in interactions with co-workers. But while her primary interest is in this 'first person' use of Kanter's archetypes, she also observes that they can be used in the third person, in representations of women. This insight can be applied to mass media representations of powerful women, including or perhaps especially female political leaders. In press coverage of GE2015, there are numerous representations which appear to draw on Kanter's archetypes, particularly the 'Iron Maiden' and the 'Seductress'.

Iron Maidens: The Representation of Female Authority

In a study of the representation of businessmen and women in English-language business magazines, Veronika Koller (2004) draws attention to the way actors in discourse may be gendered by the use of particular metaphors. For instance, in business writing, one common conceptual metaphor is BUSINESS IS WAR: within that frame, business leaders may be figured as warriors and military commanders (e.g. 'Fiorina rallied her troops'). In this case Koller found that the same metaphor was used frequently to represent both men and women—though to the extent that war is culturally coded as a male activity, this is a gendered metaphor which tends to masculinize female subjects. In other cases, however, there were differences: metaphors figuring business as a competitive sport and business leaders as athletes were more commonly used in relation to male subjects, and metaphors figuring business as service to others and businesspeople as carers were more common in reference to women.

Figurative comparisons involving politicians (taking the form of either metaphor or simile) were common in our sample of press coverage, and a particular set of comparisons recurred in descriptions of women exercising authority. This is especially striking in relation to Nicola Sturgeon, but it is also, interestingly, a salient feature of the representation of one female non-politician, the newscaster Julie Etchingham, who moderated the first TV debate. Examples (1)–(3) below relate to Etchingham and (4)–(6) relate to Sturgeon:

(1) Our Julie was also in a white jacket that gave her the air of an imperious dental nurse.

(2) Looking like a bizarre cross between Nurse Ratched from *One Flew Over the Cuckoo's Nest* and a Theresa May tribute act, she appeared on our screens.

(3) This headmistress was not taking any nonsense from the naughty boys and girls at the back of the class.

(4) But the Aussie (i.e. Natalie Bennett) backed the head girl Nicola when she took on the Prime Minister, saying: 'I agree with Nicola.'

(5) She was very much like a primary school teacher, bobbing her head up and down, using her hands a lot.

(6) She ticked off Nigel Farage like a hospital matron who has found something nasty in the ward.

Each of these examples likens its subject to the occupant of a traditionally female role which confers some kind of authority on the holder (nurse, matron, head girl, primary school teacher, headmistress). Most of these are lower-status roles than the ones Sturgeon and Etchingham actually occupy, and the authority they confer is generally of a rather limited and petty kind: head girls, teachers, and headmistresses have authority mainly over children, and rarely over adult males, while nurses have authority over adults in situations where they are temporarily disempowered by illness. Another feature the roles have in common is that the authority associated with them is often resented. The descriptions of nurses in examples (1), (2), and (6) make clear that we are dealing not with the stereotype of the nurse as ministering angel or sex object, but with the tyrannical 'battleaxe'—a version of the 'Iron Maiden'. Nurse Ratched in *One Flew Over the Cuckoo's Nest* is a classic fictional example, and popular cultural depictions of 'Matron' (e.g. in British films in the 'Carry On…' series) have generally been comic variations on the same theme (the character is typically physically unalluring but sexually voracious, as well as domineering). These comparisons inflect Kanter's 'Iron Maiden' archetype in a way that belittles Etchingham and Sturgeon, and suggests an undercurrent of resentment towards them. In the one case (example (6)), which describes a man in similarly belittling terms (the 'ticked off' Nigel Farage), the insult depends on the assumption that submission to female authority demeans men.

Here, it might be objected that these are jocular rather than serious comments: examples (1), (4), and (6) belong to the 'sketch' genre, whose aim is to entertain by making fun of politicians (the idea of the seven participants in the first debate as like unruly children in a classroom is typical of this kind of writing). Yet it must tell us something that sketch writers repeatedly reach for the figure of the 'battleaxe' when writing about women, whereas they do not make analogous comparisons when writing about men. A search for parallel expressions referring to males (e.g. 'head boy', 'headmaster', 'schoolmaster', 'doctor') produced only one result, a comment that, at times during the first debate, David Cameron had sounded like a headmaster. This did not come from a humorous item: the commenter was the same 'body language expert' who, a couple of sentences earlier, had likened Nicola Sturgeon to a primary school teacher.

This example brings to light an apparent contradiction. Since 'headmaster' is a higher-status occupation than 'primary school teacher', the obvious interpretation is that the expert found Cameron more impressive than Sturgeon. However, the piece in which the two comparisons appear makes clear that he did not: rather, he was quoted giving expert support to the article's thesis that Sturgeon had been the debate's star performer ('Can I vote for the SNP, voters ask', *Independent*, 3 April). Similarly, examples (2) and (3) are from a piece by Julia Hartley-Brewer in the *Telegraph* ('In a field of strong women, Etchingham shows she's boss', 3 April) which was clearly meant to be positive, commending Etchingham for her skilful performance as a moderator. But the use of negatively loaded cultural references produces an ambiguous or contradictory message. It is as if these variants of the 'Iron Maiden' archetype have become so natural-ized in representations of female authority that their negative and belit-tling elements pass unnoticed. For the mass media, which depend heavily on forms of cultural shorthand that readers can be expected to understand immediately, comparisons with stereotypical 'battleaxes' may be simply a default choice, made because of a lack of more positive options that have the same familiarity.

Our sample did contain several examples of a comparison which did not associate female authority with petty tyranny: a number of pieces com-pared Nicola Sturgeon to the character of Birgitte Nyborg in the Danish political TV drama *Borgen*. Nyborg is a politician who unexpectedly becomes Prime Minister in a closely fought multiparty election; she is also a rounded and sympathetic character who transcends the 'Iron Maiden' stereotype by combining intelligence, strength, and determination with emotional warmth, nurturance, and vulnerability. Sturgeon herself may have encouraged this comparison by nominating *Borgen* as her favou-rite TV programme (she was also known to have invited the actor who plays Nyborg to visit Scotland and meet her in person). References to the Danish drama appear to have acquired some resonance for the British public (they also appeared in stories framed by the 'horse race' narrative, with the multiparty campaign being said to represent 'the Borgenisation of British politics' [*Guardian*, 2 April]). But it is, perhaps, depressing that the most positive comparator for a female political leader should be a fic-tional character.

THE SEDUCTRESS: POLITICS AS SEX

The 'Iron Maiden' archetype is the most overtly powerful of the four, and it is therefore not surprising that it figures prominently in representations of female political leaders. But the 'Seductress' also appears, again mainly in representations of Nicola Sturgeon. The themes of seduction, flirting, romance, sex, and marriage are referenced in these headlines (emphasis added):

(1) She'll charm you—but don't fall for the *siren* of the SNP
(2) A *romance* for our times
(3) Coalition *flirting* steps up a gear
(4) *Bedder* or worse
(5) Ed Miliband and Nicola Sturgeon are the *George and Mildred* of politics
(6) Sturgeon tells Miliband he will *come running*

The first of these examples comes from an opinion piece in which a Scottish writer warns English voters unfamiliar with Nicola Sturgeon of the hidden danger she represents. All the other examples refer to her relationship with the Labour leader Ed Miliband, with whom the right-wing press feared the SNP might form a coalition. In these cases the underlying conceptual metaphor equates political alliances with sexual relationships, and this gives rise to a network of related but more specific metaphors (e.g. 'political advances are sexual advances' and 'a coalition is a marriage'). This is a familiar metaphor in political journalism, and it is not used only in cases where the partners are a man and a woman. It was common during the 2010 negotiations that produced the Conservative–Liberal Democrat coalition in which David Cameron served as Prime Minister and Nick Clegg as his Deputy. In that case there were jokes about the two men being like a married couple, or like the characters in a Hollywood 'bromance'. In the GE2015 case, by contrast, the female in the relationship, Nicola Sturgeon, is described in terms which were not used about Nick Clegg. She is portrayed as a version of Kanter's 'Seductress', the woman who uses her sexuality to gain influence over a more powerful man, and who aspires to be the 'power behind the throne'. Unsurprisingly, there are several references in our sample that compare Sturgeon to that classic (and Scottish) 'power behind the throne', Lady Macbeth; more prosaically, example (5) calls Miliband and Sturgeon 'the George and Mildred of politics', a reference to the 1970s TV sitcom *George and Mildred*, in which Mildred was an example of the sexually voracious 'battleaxe' and George was her long-suffering henpecked husband. This marital metaphor served a dual purpose for the Conservative press: as well as presenting Sturgeon as monstrous, it implied that Miliband was weak and naïve.

In the more extended examples reproduced below, the theme of the henpecked man and the sexually predatory woman comes even more strongly to the fore:

> Spring is the season when pigeons distract us with their mating dance. The male paces about in an exotic strut, coo-cooing and puffing out his chest. The female makes a show of mincing away from him. He follows; she side-steps; he pursues; she retreats. … On Thursday night on the BBC a similar courtship ritual could be observed taking place between two politicians, but with this striking difference. It was the lady in the dove-grey jacket coo-cooing with a puffed-out chest, and the gentleman in the dove-grey tie who was being coy. ('Nicola Sturgeon and the politics of sadism', *Times*, 18 April)

> Nicola Sturgeon may wear high heels and a skirt, but the eerie silence from noisy ex-leader Alex Salmond proves she eats her partners alive. ('Sisterhood politics won't be ladylike', *Sun*, 20 April)

The first example suggests that in the Sturgeon–Miliband partnership, it is Sturgeon who plays the active male role and Miliband who plays the passive female one—a reversal of the natural order of things. In the second example Sturgeon exemplifies the female who is deadlier than the male: she is figured as a mate-eating spider who has already seduced and consumed one man, her former boss Alex Salmond, and is poised to do the same to Ed Miliband. Though these comparisons also present Ed Miliband negatively, the depiction of a man as weak and passive does not imply the same fear and loathing as the comparison of a woman to the Siren or the Black Widow.

VOICE AND POWER: FIGURING WOMEN'S SPEECH

Another kind of covertly gendered linguistic pattern is illustrated by this example, from a sketch that appeared in the *Telegraph* after the second debate ('BBC Debate sketch', 16 April):

> "Ed Miliband is scared to be bold," *scowled* Ms Sturgeon. "We don't want a pretend alternative to austerity."

> "Exactly right!" *squeaked* Ms Bennett.

> "Labour are letting the Tories off the hook!" *snapped* Ms Wood. The audience applauded.

> Desperately Mr Miliband tried to steer the debate back to his absent foe. "Let's not pretend there's no difference between me and David Cameron," he *said*, rather pleadingly.
>
> "There's not a big enough difference!" *barked* Ms Sturgeon.

The italicized words are quotatives, verbs of speaking—except that most of them do not straightforwardly describe speech. The generic quotative verb *say* is used in relation to the only male participant in this reported exchange, Ed Miliband, while the women's contributions are reported using verbs that either index an affective stance (*scowl* and *snap*, both indicating displeasure with the addressee) or evoke aspects of voice quality (and indirectly, affect) through a metaphorical comparison with non-human vocalization (*squeak*, which denotes the noise made by a mouse or other small animal, and *bark*, the noise made by a dog).

Using non-generic quotatives that communicate more than just 'X said Y' is a common device in literary discourse, where the choice of verb may contribute to the reader's perception of a character's personality or current mood. That is also what it does in this example. It may communicate, for instance, that Nicola Sturgeon is the alpha-female of the group: she is fierce and Natalie Bennett is either timid or over-excited ('squeak' has more than one interpretation, so its meaning in context will depend on what inferences the reader makes). It may also suggest that the women's speech is more emotionally expressive than Miliband's, and—since what it expresses is displeasure—that they are ganging up on him. That interpretation may be reinforced by the use of the adverbial 'pleadingly' to describe the manner in which Miliband's words were 'said': pleading is generally addressed by someone in a powerless position to someone in a more powerful one. Miliband is once again being framed here as a henpecked male in a group of dominant females. The writer may not have made his choices with the conscious intention of communicating these meanings (and since they require inference on the part of the reader, they may or may not have been successfully communicated), but he is nevertheless following a gendered script.

GENDER, POWER, AND REPRESENTATION

What general conclusions can be drawn from this analysis of GE2015 press coverage? Was this the election where women were finally treated with the respect they deserved (cf. Ross 2015), or was it just the usual parading of sexist attitudes, words, and images (cf. Harmer 2015b; Savigny 2015)?

We would argue that it was a mixture of both. On the basic question of women's media presence, we have suggested that the figures produced by quantitative analysis should not be taken automatically as evidence of a direct gender bias. The predominance of men was rather the by-product of a 'presidential' bias which favoured leaders over non-leaders, and leaders who might become prime minister over other leaders. This produced female winners as well as losers. The women most obviously marginalized by it were the senior female members of the main parties, like Theresa May and Harriet Harman. Men of comparable (but not greater) stature, like George Osborne and Ed Balls, did have more media visibility, according to Loughborough's calculations, and that may indicate a more direct gender bias. However, the focus on leaders (more specifically, on those who participated in the TV debates) clearly boosted the visibility of the three party leaders who were women. Without it, Bennett and Wood would have struggled to attract national attention, and while Sturgeon would probably have had some presence, she would not have been the dominant figure she ultimately became. The way the debates were set up gave all three women a public voice which no woman has had in a UK General Election campaign since Margaret Thatcher. The second debate, which Cameron and Clegg did not participate in, offered British viewers the unprecedented spectacle of a major national political event at which women speakers outnumbered men.

The rise of 'the women' was itself a theme in GE2015 press coverage, with most commentators hailing it as a positive development, and some going so far as to suggest it was the most significant feature of the entire campaign. Beneath this overt enthusiasm, though, the rhetoric of the press often covertly reinscribed stereotypical, sexist, and on occasion misogynistic propositions about women. On the one hand, they were nicer than men, and offered a fresh, modern alternative to the 'identikit' members of the 'Westminster boys' club'; on the other, they were a 'scarlet sisterhood' of battleaxes, oddballs, silly girls, and dangerous power-crazed man-eaters.

While we agree with Karen Ross (2015) that the attacks made on Nicola Sturgeon were, in part, a mark of her opponents' respect for her, we are sceptical about the suggestion that changing public attitudes have made sexism in itself less acceptable or less 'relevant'. Arguably what has shifted is rather the form in which sexist media representations are most commonly packaged. As we noted in our discussion of the use of the 'battleaxe' figure, many instances of sexism in our sample come from genres of newspaper writing which are either explicitly flagged as satirical/humorous (like sketches and cartoons) or else foreground the writer's personal viewpoint (like columns and opinion pieces). These kinds of writing occupy more space in newspapers—especially the upmarket or 'quality' titles—than they did in the past, and they give writers a license to practise what has been called 'sexism with an alibi' (Williamson 2003). In advertising, the main focus of Williamson's analysis, the alibi is often what she labels 'retrosexism', the location of a sexist scenario in a 'period' frame, so that criticism can be deflected by saying, in effect, 'but everyone knows women are equal now'. Retrosexism is a variant of the larger phenomenon of 'post-feminism', in which the alibi for sexism is irony or 'citationality': you are not actually doing sexism, you are citing it ironically, making fun of it in a cool, postmodern way. Many of the sexist comments we have quoted from opinion pieces would fall into this 'ironic' category. 'Matron' and the other battleaxes are 'retro' stereotypes; even the *Sun*'s crude efforts might be defended as a visual analogue of 'banter'—sexism and sexual harassment passed off as 'just a bit of fun'. And this packaging makes sexism difficult to challenge, because the challenger will come across as humourless and uncool.

Another post-feminist alibi for sexism is the idea that it now affects men and women equally. We have noted in this chapter that press coverage of GE2015 represented men in some of the same ways that have long prompted complaints of sexism from women. Judgements were made on their physical appearance and taste in clothes (and even shoes). Their marital and domestic arrangements were discussed, and their kitchen décor was debated. There was even some sexual objectification of men in the 'Milifandom' campaign. However, we have argued that this is not simply 'the same thing' regardless of whether the target is male or female. As Williamson (2003) points out, 'the notion of gender "equality" within sexual imagery takes no account of gender inequality in the world surrounding it'. Some of the ways in which men were trivialized and mocked by the press (e.g. using the figure of the henpecked husband or the naughty schoolboy) depend on the assumption of gender inequality: what makes men appear weak or ridiculous is allowing women to have power over them.

The idea of women's 'different voice' recurred in commentary on the TV debates, and was typically framed by the more general, overtly positive discourse on women in politics to which we referred above. But if we compare media commentary on the female party leaders' speech styles with the analysis presented in Chap. 2, it is evident that there is a gap between the representation and the reality of the women's verbal behaviour. Our analysis showed very few clear-cut gender differences in communication style: a similar range of strategies, including both adversarial and supportive moves, was deployed by both male and female leaders. The idea that women are more considerate of others' speaking rights, that they do not generally interrupt or talk over others or continue to hold the floor in defiance of requests to cede it, is not borne out by the data examined in Chap. 2. The sequence reproduced as Extract 5, for instance (p. 54), shows Nicola Sturgeon employing interruption and simultaneous talk to build a sustained attack on Ed Miliband. Her repertoire also included other strategies (such as the use of sarcastic wisecracks) which are commonly associated with 'male' performance styles. Leanne Wood made some bold adversarial moves (like hijacking a turn already allocated to someone else), which challenge the media's presentation of her as 'softer' and more 'feminine' than the other women. Conversely, our analysis did not bear out the assumption that men's rhetoric is less personal or relational than women's: in these debates it was the men who were more likely to refer to their experiences as spouses and parents.

On the other hand, our analysis reveals individual differences which were glossed over in commentary opposing 'the women' to 'the men'. Natalie Bennett and Nigel Farage stand out from their colleagues, both in their respective gender categories and overall: both sometimes used strategies (such as shouting) which the other leaders avoided, while making less frequent or less effective use of strategies that were common to all participants. Bennett rarely improvised and took very few uninvited turns; Farage took many uninvited turns but was often unsuccessful in using these interventions to gain and then keep the floor. Though many commentators asserted that the first debate was 'won' by 'the women', there was actually a considerable gap between Sturgeon's noticeably effective performance and Bennett's much less assured one. Similarly, there was an obvious contrast between Farage's performance and Cameron's.

Overall, the analysis we have presented in this chapter points to two general conclusions. The first is that the reception of women's political speech in GE2015 was shaped to a significant extent by the 'different voice' ideology. Some assessments (particularly those that focused on Nicola Sturgeon as an individual) did depart from this framing, but commentary which explicitly rejected or challenged it was rare. If we set the media's representation of the two televised debates alongside our earlier analysis of these speech events, we would argue that the verbal behaviour of male and female politicians was more strongly gendered in reception than it was in production. The women were persistently represented as more different from the men than they really were, and what was said about the nature of the differences often owed more to familiar gender stereotypes than to careful observations of the behaviour being commented on.

Our second general conclusion is that discourse not only on gender and language but also more broadly on gender and power, authority and leadership, continues to put women at a disadvantage in the public sphere, creating contradictions and conflicts which are difficult to negotiate successfully. The argument made by Lünenborg and Maier (2015) in their analysis of the German press's treatment of Angela Merkel is also applicable to the British press's treatment of women in the GE2015 campaign: '[I]t is possible for female politicians to gain recognition, but this recognition remains within the logic of a gendered system.'

REFERENCES

Baxter, J. (2012). Women of the corporation: A sociolinguistic perspective of senior women's leadership language in the UK. *Journal of Sociolinguistics, 16*(1), 81–107.

Beckett, C. (2015). The battle for the stage: Broadcasting. In P. Cowley & D. Kavanagh (Eds.), *The British General Election of 2015* (pp. 278–301). Basingstoke, Hampshire: Palgrave Macmillan.

Cammaerts, B. (2015). Did Britain's right-wing newspapers win it for the Tories? *LSE GE2015*, May 13 [online]. http://blogs.lse.ac.uk/generalelection/is-it-the-daily-hate-co-wot-won-it/. Accessed 26 September 2015.

Carlin, D. B., & Winfrey, K. L. (2009). Have you come a long way, baby? Hillary Clinton, Sarah Palin and sexism in 2008 campaign coverage. *Communication Studies, 60*(4), 326–343.

Cushion, S., & Sambrook, R. (2015). The "horse race" contest dominated TV news election coverage. In D. Jackson & E. Thorsen (Eds.), *UK election analysis 2015: Media, voters and the campaign* (p. 11). Political Studies Association/Centre for the Study of Journalism, Culture and Community, Bournemouth University.

Davies, C. E. (2015). Twitter as political discourse: The case of Sarah Palin. In J. Wilson & D. Boxer (Eds.), *Discourse, politics and women as global leaders* (pp. 93–120). Amsterdam: John Benjamins.

Esser, F. (1999). Tabloidization of news. A comparative analysis of Anglo-American and German press journalism. *European Journal of Communication, 14*(3), 291–324.

Fawcett (2015). The election campaign's invisible women, 30 April [online]. http://www.fawcettsociety.org.uk/blog/the-invisible-women-in-the-election/. Accessed 27 July 2015.

Harmer, E. (2015a). Men writing about men: Media and the UK General Election 2015 [online]. http://blog.lboro.ac.uk/general-election/men-writing-about-men-media-and-the-uk-general-election-2015/. Accessed 24 July 2015.

Harmer, E. (2015b). The right man for the job: The gendered campaign. In D. Jackson & E. Thorsen (Eds.), *UK election analysis 2015: Media, voters and the campaign* (p. 15). Political Studies Association/Centre for the Study of Journalism, Culture and Community, Bournemouth University.

Jackson, D., & Thorsen, E. (Eds.) (2015). *UK election analysis 2015: Media, voters and the campaign.* Political Studies Association/Centre for the Study of Journalism, Culture and Community, Bournemouth University

Kanter, R. M. (1993). *Men and Women of the corporation* (2nd ed.). New York: Basic Books.

Koller, V. (2004). Businesswomen and war metaphors: "Possessive, jealous and pugnacious?"'. *Journal of Sociolinguistics, 8*(1), 3–22.

Lawless, J. (2009). Sexism and gender bias in election 2008: A more complex path for women in politics. *Politics & Gender, 5*(1), 70–80.

Lewis, H. (2015). The motherhood trap. *New Statesman,* 16 July [online]. http://www.newstatesman.com/politics/2015/07/motherhood-trap. Accessed 24 July 2015.

Loughborough University Communication Research Centre. (2015). Media coverage of the 2015 campaign: Report 5 [online]. http://blog.lboro.ac.uk/general-election/media-coverage-of-the-2015-campaign-report-5/. Accessed 24 July 2015.

Lünenborg, M., & Maier, T. (2015). Governing in the gendered structure of power: The media discourse on Angela Merkel and her power-driven leadership style. In J. Wilson & D. Boxer (Eds.), *Discourse, politics and women as global leaders* (pp. 275–292). Amsterdam: John Benjamins.

Mäkelä, J., Isotalus, P., & Ruoho, I. (2015). The ball is in the women's court: The portrayal of women as political leaders in Finnish newspapers. In J. Wilson & D. Boxer (Eds.), *Discourse, politics and women as global leaders* (pp. 293–314). Amsterdam: John Benjamins.

Margetts, H., & Hale, S. (2015). Digital disconnect: Parties, pollsters and political analysis in #GE2015. *Elections and the Internet: Research from the Oxford Internet Institute,* 12 May [online]. http://elections.oii.ox.ac.uk/digital-disconnect-parties-pollsters-and-political-analysis-in-ge2015/. Accessed 26 September.

McLachlan, S., & Golding, P. (2000). Tabloidization in the British Press: A quantitative investigation into changes in British newspapers, 1952-1987. In C. Sparks & J. Tulloch (Eds.), *Tabloid tales: Global debates over media standards.* New York: Rowman and Littlefield.

Meeks, L. (2012). Is she "Man Enough"? Women candidates, executive political offices, and news coverage. *Journal of Communication, 62,* 175–193.

Meeks, L. (2013). All the gender that fit to print: How the *New York Times* covered Hillary Clinton and Sarah Palin in 2008. *Journalism & Mass Communication Quarterly, 90*(3), 520–539.

Ross, K. (2015). Girls on top, who knew? The unpredictability of pollsters and publics. In D. Jackson & E. Thorsen (Eds.), *UK election analysis 2015: Media, voters and the campaign* (p. 18). Political Studies Association/Centre for the Study of Journalism, Culture and Community, Bournemouth University.

Savigny, H. (2015). Why can't I vote for a female candidate? In D. Jackson & E. Thorsen (Eds.), *UK election analysis 2015: Media, voters and the campaign* (p. 19). Political Studies Association/Centre for the Study of Journalism, Culture and Community, Bournemouth University.

Semetko, H. A., & Boomgaarden, H. G. (2007). Reporting Germany's 2005 Bundestag Election Campaign: Was gender an issue? *The Harvard International Journal of Press/Politics, 12* (4), 154–171.

Wahl-Jorgensen, K. (2015). The kitchen as the new campaign battleground: Changing notions of masculinity. In D. Jackson & E. Thorsen (Eds.), *UK election analysis 2015: Media, voters and the campaign* (p. 24). Political Studies Association/Centre for the Study of Journalism, Culture and Community, Bournemouth University.

Williamson, J. (2003). Sexism with an alibi. *Guardian*, 31 May [online]. http://www.theguardian.com/media/2003/may/31/advertising.comment. Accessed 6 September 2015.

CHAPTER 4

Conclusions

Abstract This concluding chapter draws together the strands of our case study and considers what it contributes to the study of gender, language, and politics. It begins by revisiting the case study's central questions: how the female party leaders used language in the televised GE2015 leaders' debates, and how their behaviour related to the familiar ideological representation of women's 'different voice'. We then discuss the debates as media events, in which participants designed their performances for a national television audience. We consider some evidence about the way they were perceived by 'ordinary' viewers, and take a closer look at how one of the women, Nicola Sturgeon, successfully negotiated the demand for politicians to be both 'articulate' and 'authentic'.

Keywords Articulacy • Authenticity • Media discourse • Nicola Sturgeon • Nigel Farage

INTRODUCTION

At the beginning of this book, we asked: 'What does it mean, concretely, to say that women speak a different political language, and how far do descriptions of that language...correspond to women's actual behaviour in political settings?' (p. 4). In fact, the claim that women have a different

© The Editor(s) (if applicable) and The Author(s) 2016   113
D. Cameron, S. Shaw, *Gender, Power and Political Speech*,
DOI 10.1057/978-1-137-58752-7_4

way of speaking, though it recurs across a range of sources (academic articles, media commentary, interviews with female politicians themselves),
is rarely couched in concrete descriptive terms. Rather than describing its
distinctive characteristics, many references to it simply contrast it with an
implied male norm. Women are depicted as 'more cooperative' or 'less
combative and aggressive'; they are said to eschew such stereotypically
male behaviours as shouting, interrupting, talking over opponents, getting
involved in heated arguments or exchanges of insults. Women's speech is
defined largely through assertions about what it is not, and this tells us
very little about what it actually is. In fact, both the men and the women
evoked by statements like 'women are less combative' are stereotypes—
idealized representations which do not capture the complexity of real-
world linguistic practice.

Gender and Speech Style: Is There a 'Different Voice'?

As we showed in Chap. 2, the actual female politicians who participated in
the GE2015 debates did not eschew the competitive and assertive behaviours whose avoidance is often cited as a defining characteristic of wom-
en's 'different voice'. They did sometimes raise their voices (in Natalie
Bennett's case, to a level extreme enough to make it headline news), and
while they were rarely involved in the most heated two-way exchanges,
they were not averse to engaging in arguments with their opponents.
Wood and Sturgeon were quicker than their male colleagues to take issue
with Farage's comments on immigrants in the first debate, while in the
second, Sturgeon goaded Farage with a series of sarcastic and mocking
comments (Chap. 2, Extract 12). Sturgeon also persistently challenged
Miliband, often by interrupting or speaking simultaneously with him
(Chap. 2, Extracts 4 and 5). Interruption was a strategy used by all participants (Chap. 2, Figs. 2.7 and 2.13), and women were responsible for
some of the most 'aggravated' examples (those which violated an opponent's speaking rights most overtly). Women also challenged the authority
of the moderators by speaking, or continuing to speak, when the floor had
already been allocated to someone else.

Another observation that is often made about women's 'different
voice', in scholarly work as well as popular discussions, is that women's
preference for collaborative and egalitarian forms of interaction, and their

corresponding dislike of competition, contributes to disadvantaging them in situations where participants must compete to gain and hold the floor (e.g. Karpowitz and Mendelberg 2014). It is true that in the GE2015 debates, the women, overall, spoke less than the men. In the first debate, all the four male participants took more speaking time than any of the three female ones. In the second, where women outnumbered men, both the men present spoke for more time than two out of the three women, and one (Miliband) spoke for more time than any of them (the other, Farage, got slightly less time than Nicola Sturgeon, but the difference, in a ninety-minute debate, was only just over a minute). However, gendered stylistic preferences are not the only factor that might be relevant to the explanation of this pattern. As we pointed out in Chap. 2, the distribution of speaking time in a debate does not only reflect participants' own behaviour (their willingness or otherwise to seize the floor when opportunities arise, and their ability to keep control of it), but also the way they are treated by other participants and by the moderator. This, in turn, reflects differences of status which are not primarily about gender, though they may be indirectly linked to it.

In Edelsky and Adams's classic study of US gubernatorial debates (1990), incumbency, party affiliation, and political experience were all found to advantage speakers in competition for the floor, and since these forms of status were not equally distributed among male and female candidates, the result was that 'men got better treatment (safer turn spaces, extra turns, follow ups on their topics)' (Edelsky and Adams 1990: 186). In the GE2015 debates, similarly, men were allocated more invited and thus 'secure' turns, and given more opportunities to respond to others' points; but not all the men benefited equally from this 'better treatment'. In the ITV debate, the beneficiaries were the two incumbents (i.e. the leaders of the coalition government parties) and the leader of the main opposition party, Ed Miliband; in the BBC debate, from which incumbents were excluded, the moderator's management of the floor gave a clear advantage to Miliband, the leader of the largest party among the challengers. Of course, it is impossible to say with certainty that the same patterns would have been obtained if the position occupied in the first debate by Cameron, or in the second by Miliband, had instead been filled by a woman. But on balance we think it is reasonable to posit that these patterns were more directly related to other kinds of status (incumbency and party affiliation) than to gender in and of itself.

Popular versions of the 'different voice' ideology depict women as cooperative and supportive language users; in commentary on the debates, it was often noted that the three female party leaders behaved supportively towards each other. In Chap. 2, we suggested that this did not preclude competition between them (see Extract 13), but it is nevertheless fair to say that their behaviour towards each other was more supportive than their behaviour towards the male leaders. None of them directly challenged or argued with a female co-participant; all of them voiced agreement with another woman's contribution on at least one occasion. Once again, though, it is not obvious that the most convincing explanation for this relates to gendered stylistic preferences (or to feminist solidarity, though that may also have been a factor). The women had tactical reasons for cooperating rather than competing: by supporting each other, they strengthened the main political message their three parties had in common, that there was an alternative to the austerity policies put forward by all the other parties. Conversely, they had nothing to gain from arguing with each other, because their parties were not in competition for the same voters. In the case of Wood and Sturgeon, the overlap was zero, since Plaid Cymru was only contesting the election in Wales, while the SNP was only contesting it in Scotland. In both cases, the opponent they needed to defeat on their home territory was Labour. There is no reason to think that Sturgeon would have behaved any more supportively to a female Labour leader than she behaved towards Ed Miliband. In fact, there is a reason to think otherwise.

In the Scottish Parliament, the political contest between the ruling SNP, led by Sturgeon, and the Labour opposition, led by Kezia Dugdale, is regularly played out at 'First Minister's Questions' (FMQs). This event is analogous to 'Prime Minister's Questions' (PMQs) at Westminster: though in both assemblies its nominal purpose is to allow elected members to interrogate the government by putting a series of questions to its chief (Prime or First) minister, in practice it is understood to be a confrontation between the two main party leaders, in which the Leader of the Opposition attacks the government's record and the Prime/First Minister defends it, typically in a manner that allows him or her to make counterattacks on the opposing party. Since these exchanges epitomize the adversarial 'Punch and Judy politics' which women are said to find alien and off-putting, we might expect their most confrontational features to be toned down in exchanges between a female First Minister and a female opposition leader. But, in fact, the two women have maintained the traditional, extremely adversarial character of the occasion. Here, we reproduce an extract from FMQs on 17 September 2015:

Extract 14

NS=Nicola Sturgeon (SNP) KD = Kezia Dugdale (Lab) PO = Presiding Officer (Tricia Marwick) MSP= member of the Scottish Parliament

1   NS: (end of turn) when it comes to education (.) when it comes to <u>health</u>(.) when it

2   comes to <u>jus</u>tice and getting <u>crime</u> levels down to a forty-one year <u>low</u>(.) I'll

3   leave <u>La</u>bour to(.)to coin a phrase from Kezia Dugdale (.) <u>carp</u>from the si<u>de</u>lines

4   (.)⌐ I will get on with delivering⌐ the <u>ac</u>tion that the people of Scotland

5   MSPs: └laughter 2 seconds   ┘

6   NS: need and de<u>serve</u>

7   MSPs:⌐Applause 5 seconds   ┐

8   PO: └Kezia <u>Dug</u>dale (.) Miss <u>Dug</u>dale┘

9   KD: the First Minister mentions the polls let us <u>talk</u> about the <u>polls</u> (.) <u>she</u> might be

10   popular in them (.) but her record on education <u>isn't</u> (.)⌐ just <u>one</u> in <u>three</u> (.) ┐

11   MSPs: └Applause 2 seconds┘

12   KD: just <u>one</u> in three people in Scotland think your record on education is up to

13   scratch and if <u>you</u> are proud of that (.) <u>great</u> (.) but don't expect any

14   congratulations from me you can turn and the back benchers will clap you but

15   just one in three people think you've got a good record when it comes to

16   education⌐(3)   ┐

17   MSPs   └Applause 3 seconds┘

18   KD: here's the thing Presiding Officer this is the First Minister who promised us not

19   so long a<u>go</u> (.) that the referendum was a <u>once</u> in a generation event (.) now she

20   has a <u>shopp</u>ing list of material changes that she thinks will justify another

21   referendum (.) instead of using the full force of government (.) to make a

22   difference to the lives of young Scots (.) the SNP want

23   ⎰ us to go through the same arguments all over again (.)⎱

24   MSPs:⎱ Loud talking   ⎰

25   PO: order

26   KD: in Scotland today you are twice as likely to get an A in your highers if you go to

27   private school than if you go to state school and we know that a young person

28   from a rich background is twice as likely to go on to higher education as someone

29   from a poor background (.) she has had eight years (.) so can I ask her (.) when

30   will the First Minister deliver a material change in the number of poorer children

31   going to higher education⎰(3)   ⎱

32   MSPs: ⎱Applause 3 seconds⎰

33   PO: First Minister (.) First Minister

34   NS: well (.) Kezia Dugdale clearly could not decide whether she wanted to ask about

35   education or about independence (.) maybe she should have followed the

36   example of her new leader and asked the audience what she should have asked

37   about today (turn continues)

This extract begins with Sturgeon defending the SNP's record in office and suggesting that the Labour opposition are just 'carping from the sidelines' (line 3). Dugdale then homes in on a specific issue—inequality of access to higher education—where independent research suggests the situation has worsened under the SNP. In criticizing Sturgeon's record on this issue, Dugdale also reiterates a common complaint among the SNP's opponents, that the nationalists are neglecting problems like educational inequality because the only thing they really care about is creating the conditions for a further referendum on Scottish independence. Rather than answering the question that Dugdale ends by posing ('when is she going to deliver a material change in the number of poorer children who are going to higher education?'[lines 29–31]), Sturgeon responds by accusing Dugdale of not knowing what she wants to ask about, education or independence. She refuses to be put on the defensive, and instead goes on the offensive by attacking the competence of her questioner.

Sturgeon's final remark in the previous extract (lines 34–37) is effectively a meta-comment on how leaders should conduct political exchanges. 'Maybe she should have followed the example of her new leader' is a reference to Jeremy Corbyn, who succeeded Ed Miliband as the national leader of the Labour Party in September 2015. On his first appearance at PMQs as Leader of the Opposition, Corbyn said that the ordinary people he had met during his campaign were alienated by the 'theatricality' of PMQs: they wanted it to be more accessible and more relevant to their concerns. He proceeded to ask David Cameron a series of questions which had been submitted by members of the public. Sturgeon alludes to this departure from convention in her suggestion that perhaps Dugdale should have 'asked the audience what she should ask about today' (lines 36 and 37). Since she makes this suggestion while attacking Dugdale for not knowing her own mind, she appears to be implying that she regards Corbyn's approach as weak and indecisive.

Both Sturgeon and Dugdale appear very comfortable with the traditional approach, in which most 'questions' are pretexts for attacking the First Minister and her administration, and most 'answers' are counter-attacks directed against the Labour leader and her party. The robustness of their exchanges is interesting, not only because these are exchanges between two women, but also because they take place in a political assembly where female leadership has become normalized. Sturgeon is the first woman to serve as Scotland's First Minister, but she is not the first to lead a political party in the Scottish Parliament: since the institution opened in 1999, five women have led their parties, and the election of Dugdale as Scottish Labour leader after GE2015 brought the number serving concurrently to three (Sturgeon, Dugdale, and the Conservative Ruth Davidson). In this context it becomes difficult to make the argument which is sometimes made about women at Westminster—that they feel compelled to adopt a hyper-combative style to hold their own with powerful men or to demonstrate their 'insider' status. Sturgeon, with the advantages of incumbency and long experience, is in a particularly strong position to change the rules of engagement and set a different tone at FMQs, but she evidently prefers the combative style illustrated by the previous extract.

In itself, of course, the existence of combative female political speakers like Sturgeon and Dugdale, or of men like Corbyn who prefer a less adversarial approach, does not refute the claim that women as a group incline more to collaborative or consensus-based styles of discourse.

(Though we should repeat that we do not regard that claim as proven beyond question, either: as we noted in Chap. 1, much of the evidence put forward to support it comes from interviews in which women describe their own speech styles, and these self-reports do not always match their observed behaviour.) However, the fact that women choose to behave combatively in settings like the Scottish Parliament, where they are not isolated and powerless 'interlopers' in an arena overwhelmingly dominated by men, must surely challenge one of the core beliefs associated with the 'different voice' ideology—that women's presence in sufficient numbers, or in influential positions, will automatically change the language of politics.

Addressing the Audience: Articulacy and Authenticity

Unlike the women MPs in Shaw's research on the House of Commons (2000; 2006), the women who participated in the GE2015 debates did not appear to be constrained by a sense of themselves as 'interlopers'. Arguably, the distinction between 'insiders' and 'interlopers', so useful for our understanding of women's position in other institutional contexts, has far less relevance, or maybe none at all, for the behaviour of participants in a televised debate. Participants in a televised debate are not joining an established institution whose rules and traditions they must demonstrate their respect for: rather, they are forming a new, temporary community of practice, subject to rules which are specific to the occasion (the 'tradition' of leaders' debates has only existed in the UK since 2010, when the format was different, and when only two of the seven 2015 participants were involved). Also, and perhaps most significantly, they are not designing their performances to be judged by other 'insiders'. Rather, they are addressing a mass audience through the medium of television.

The fact that the debates are examples of mediated political discourse differentiates our case study from much of the work cited in earlier chapters, which examined the relationship between gender and linguistic behaviour in other kinds of institutional settings (e.g. Baxter 2010; Holmes 2006; Karpowitz and Mendelberg 2014; McDowell 2015; McElhinny 1995; Shaw 2006; Walsh 2001). Studies of professional or workplace interaction tend to focus on the way men and women construct identities and negotiate relationships within the community of practice itself (e.g. a project team, a board of directors, or a school board); typically, these are groups whose members interact regularly in order to accomplish collective goals. This leads researchers to focus on questions such as how participants negotiate joint decision-making and problem-solving or how they foster solidary relations within the group and resolve interpersonal conflict. In our case study, by contrast, those are not the most salient issues. While participants in a televised debate do also construct identities and negotiate relationships, the conditions in which they do so are very different—partly because of the nature of the debate as a genre, but also because of the effects of mediation.

Unlike the participants in a workplace meeting or a small group discussion, the participants in a political debate are positioned as adversaries: they are not required to work cooperatively or make joint decisions, and they need not try to avoid or minimize conflict (on the contrary, in fact, the genre presupposes conflict and allows for its open expression). The perceptions they are most concerned to manage are not those of their fellow-debaters, but those of the audience watching the debate. This is further complicated in the case of a televised election debate by the existence of more than one audience. Participants are performing not only for the audience which is co-present with them in the studio, but also, and in fact more importantly, for the unseen, much larger audience which is watching the debate on television. This makes televised election debates different not only from team meetings and group discussions, but also from Parliamentary debates or other set-piece political events like PMQs/FMQs, where politicians design their performances primarily for an audience of insiders: though these events are also televised, they are not staged specifically to be broadcast, and members of the public who choose to watch them on television are more like 'overhearers' than direct addressees (Bell 1984). Televised election debates, by contrast, are media events: their purpose is to inform prospective voters, and participants design their performances primarily for the 'viewers at home'.

Participants in a debate do also, of course, construct relationships with one another, especially during the 'free-flowing' segments which allow them to interact directly, but it is clear that the stances they adopt towards co-participants reflect calculations about how these will 'play' with the audience. For instance, Wood, Sturgeon, and Miliband all seem to have calculated that attacking Nigel Farage would not meet with general disapproval, whereas Miliband had to be more circumspect in his arguments with Sturgeon: in most cases, 'punching down'—attacking an opponent who has less status than you do—carries the risk that you will be perceived as a bully. (This may also be a reason why the men left it to Wood and Sturgeon to condemn Farage's comments on immigrants with HIV in the first debate—a decision for which some media commentators criticized them, as we noted in Chap. 3.) Farage's attack on the 'left-wing' BBC studio audience suggests that he was designing his performance not only for viewers outside the studio, but more specifically for the subsection of the population whose political views were close to his own.

The media commentary we analysed in Chap. 3 gave some insight into how the party leaders' performances were received and evaluated, but as we pointed out, the assessments made by press commentators cannot be taken as representative of the judgements made by the public at large. Press commentary is significant because of its power to shape, in Cammaerts's (2015) phrase, 'the contours of public debate', but analysing it does not stand in for other kinds of audience research. At this point, therefore, it is of interest to look at some preliminary but suggestive evidence drawn from the Qualitative Election Survey of Britain, whose researchers Kristi Winters and Edzia Carvalho (2015) carried out research on viewers' perceptions of the party leaders shortly after the debates took place.

Their starting point was a poll (TNS Global 2015) in which 1200 respondents were asked to indicate whether their opinion of the leaders was positive or negative. An approval rating was then calculated for each leader by subtracting the percentage of negative responses from the percentage of positive ones. The highest rating (+33) went to Nicola Sturgeon, and the next highest (+12) to Nigel Farage. David Cameron (+7) was the only other leader with a positive rating: Miliband's was –8 and Clegg's –22. Intrigued by the high ratings given to two leaders who were both different in personality and poles apart politically, Winters and Carvalho set out to explore the basis for people's judgements in more depth by conducting a series of focus group discussions in England, Scotland, and Wales. From these data they concluded that group members assessed leaders' performances on two main dimensions, which they label 'articulacy' and 'authenticity'. Sturgeon and Farage stood out from the rest because they were perceived as both articulate and authentic. Miliband, Clegg, and Cameron were seen as articulate but not authentic, while Wood and Bennett were seen as authentic but not articulate.

Judgements on the 'articulacy' dimension related to a leader's perceived ability to make clear, strong, and well-reasoned arguments—an ability which was positively evaluated even where people did not agree with the arguments themselves. For instance, a focus group member in Wales who strongly disagreed with the SNP's policy of not renewing Trident, Britain's independent nuclear deterrent, nevertheless commended Sturgeon for giving a clear and well-thought-out explanation of the party's views on defence. Conversely, some people who were sympathetic to the Green Party were critical of Natalie Bennett: they felt her arguments were idealistic and lacking in practical detail, and that consequently she did not come across as a credible leader. Judgements on the 'authenticity' dimension, on the other hand, related to a leader's perceived honesty, sincerity, and lack of artifice. Leaders were judged positively where they were seen to be expressing their own beliefs in their own words, rather than falling back on stock responses or parroting lines they had been coached to produce by spin-doctors. Whereas Miliband was criticized for giving what sounded like pre-prepared answers to audience members' questions, and for using formulas like 'let me explain' repeatedly, Farage was praised for avoiding formulaic 'politician-speak'. Focus group members who were sympathetic to UKIP felt he was giving voice to what many voters really thought, but even those who were not sympathetic agreed that he spoke the language of ordinary people. Sturgeon benefited from a similar perception that she spoke straightforwardly and from personal conviction. The words 'strong' and 'passionate' recurred in the focus groups' comments about her.

Winters and Carvalho's categories of 'articulacy' and 'authenticity' bear some resemblance to the ideas of 'authority' and 'likeability' which we discussed in Chap. 1. In particular, the notion of 'articulacy' that emerged from the focus group discussions seems close to the conception of 'authority' used by scholars like Karpowitz and Mendelberg (2014); the relationship between 'authenticity' and 'likeability' is less close (though there does appear to be a connection between their negative poles in that one commonly proffered reason for disliking politicians is their perceived lack of authenticity). The focus groups' preference for leaders they perceived as both 'articulate' and 'authentic' might also remind us of the modern ideal of leadership which we described as 'encompass[ing] both traditionally "masculine" qualities (such as the ability to project authority and score points in adversarial exchanges) and the "feminine" capacity to forge connections with others and express emotion in a way that feels "sincere" and "authentic"' (p. 16). In our discussion of this ideal, we suggested that although it is in principle 'androgynous', a mixture of 'male' and 'female' elements, in practice, it is men who are more likely to be judged as exemplifying it. Research evidence suggests that women are often judged as lacking in authority, and when they are judged to display authority, it is difficult

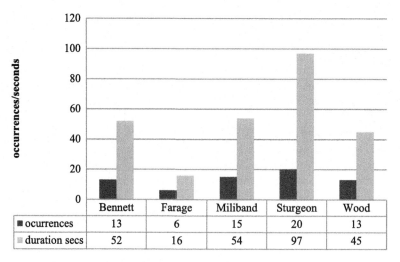

	Bennett	Farage	Miliband	Sturgeon	Wood
▪ ocurrences	13	6	15	20	13
░ duration secs	52	16	54	97	45

Fig. 4.1   Applause and laughter in the BBC debate

for them also to be perceived as likeable. In the light of this, it is not surprising that two of the women in the GE2015 debates, Natalie Bennett
and Leanne Wood, were considered by focus groups to be more 'authentic' but less 'articulate' (aka 'authoritative') than the men who took part.
But it is interesting that another woman, Nicola Sturgeon, was judged
closer to the 'articulate and authentic' ideal than any of the other leaders.

This positive judgement of Sturgeon was echoed by many media commentators, as we noted in Chap. 3, and there is some evidence that it was
also shared by the immediate audience for the debates (the people gathered
in the studio, who—in spite of Nigel Farage's accusations—were selected
to include supporters of all the parties). Sturgeon received more affiliative
responses—applause and laughter—than any of the other leaders, including those who spoke for longer overall than she did. Figure 4.1 shows how
many occurrences of applause and laughter each participant attracted during the second debate,[1] and how many seconds these affiliative responses
occupied in total (which will serve as a very rough measure of the intensity
of the response).

[1] We focus on the BBC debate here because affiliative responses in the ITV debate were
extremely few and brief: it appears that audience reaction was actively discouraged.

This chart shows that among the five challengers in the debate, Sturgeon's contributions drew the most positive reactions. But what was it about Sturgeon's performance that led audiences to perceive her so positively? And where—if anywhere—was gender in the mix?

THE PERFORMANCE OF NICOLA STURGEON

Sturgeon's performance in the debates was 'articulate' in a number of senses of that term. She spoke fluently (whereas some media commentary described Bennett's speech as 'halting' and Wood's as slow-paced), and she demonstrated her command of a range of registers, from the conversational to the markedly rhetorical. In the prepared parts of the debate, her rhetoric was quite traditional, often deploying the techniques described in Max Atkinson's classic dissection of political speech-making, *Our Masters' Voices* (1984), like the use of two-part contrasts and three-part lists, 'them versus us' references, and so on. As an illustration, consider this extract from her closing statement in the first debate, laid out and numbered to show different levels of structure and the way contrasts and lists are used:

Extract 15

1. tonight the choice at this election has been clear

    a. you can vote for the same old parties and get the same

       (i) same old politics (ii) more cuts and (iii) more misguided priorities

    b. or you can vote for something (i) different (ii) better and (iii) more

       progressive

2. I am going into this election with a clear message

    a. none of us can afford more austerity

    b. none of us can afford an additional 30 billion pounds of cuts

    c. and none can afford the 100 billion pounds that the Tories Labour and

       Liberals intend to spend on new nuclear weapons

3. their priorities are wrong

    a. but they won't pay the price

    b. it will be ordinary people across the country who pay the price

The closing statements of the other leaders in the same debate made less consistent use of these rhetorical devices. Cameron's statement was perhaps the most similar to Sturgeon's, containing two prominent examples of the well-crafted three-part list: 'We've created two million jobs...we've cut the deficit in half...we've invested in our National Health Service', and 'security for you, for your family and for our country'. The use of a 'rhetorical' style projects a certain gravitas: Winters and Carvalho (2015) found that Cameron got credit from the focus groups for sounding appropriately prime ministerial. Nicola Sturgeon's use of this style at certain points in the debates contributed to presenting her as a political leader of some consequence, the Scottish equivalent of Cameron, and she took other opportunities to remind the audience that she too was the chief minister in a national government. Responding to a question from a young woman in the audience, who pointed out that today's students have to pay for higher education and will have less job security than previous generations, Sturgeon said:

Extract 16

well I'm the First Minister of Scotland we're investing in record number of

apprenticeships (.) more affordable homes and helping (.) the poorest young

people in our country stay on at school and college but we've also kept access to

university free of tuition fees

Replying to a question about the NHS, she said:

Extract 17

I was Scottish health secretary for five years

In Scotland we've protected the budget of the NHS and we will always do so

In constructing herself as a credible leader with authority and experience, Sturgeon had an advantage over the other challengers in that she could talk about what her administration had already done or was in the process of doing, rather than just what it would do if elected. However, she also exploited the fact that for the purposes of this national election debate, she was not an incumbent, nor the most important of the challengers. Whereas higher-status participants had to be careful to avoid giving the impression of bullying lower-status opponents, Sturgeon as a small party leader was one of the 'underdogs', able to challenge anyone except for Wood and Bennett (who she had no interest in challenging anyway), without running the same risk. In Chap. 2 we saw that she was active and persistent in challenging Miliband, in particular, and that she used wisecracks and asides when criticizing Farage. If her prepared statements and references to her position in Scotland communicated authority and experience, these more spontaneous interventions communicated confidence, combativeness, and skill in arguing a point.

One media commentator we quoted in Chap. 3 said that Sturgeon was 'combative without seeming aggressive'. As we commented, this is a difficult trick for a woman to pull off, though it is also one women in leadership positions often feel called upon to attempt, since they are well aware of the tendency for female authority to be resented. In her work on the linguistic behaviour of British female senior managers, Judith Baxter (2011; 2014) has drawn attention to women's use of what she calls 'double-voiced discourse', a way of speaking that anticipates the possibility of negative judgements by showing heightened awareness of or concern for others' perceptions (the strategies her sample of businesswomen used included prefacing potentially contentious moves with apologies, or using humour and self-deprecation to mitigate the perceived assertiveness of their contributions). In mediated discourse, designed for an audience of unseen strangers, speakers are not in a position to do what Baxter describes in settings like boardrooms—adjust their behaviour from moment to moment in the light of what they know are their interlocutors' concerns or what they can see are their interlocutors' reactions. But they can try to combine ways of speaking that signal authority, confidence, and combativeness with ways of speaking that steer the audience away from the potentially negative interpretations of those qualities so that viewers will not perceive, say, authority as bossiness, confidence as arrogance, and combativeness as aggression.

We noted above that Nicola Sturgeon established authority and credibility through references to her position of power in Scotland. She also, however, described herself in other ways. In Extract 16 we reproduced the beginning of her answer to the questioner who said that young people today face rising university tuition costs along with poorer job prospects.

This opening move lists various things which Sturgeon's SNP administration in Scotland has done to help young people. But then she continues with a more personal response:

Extract 18

> I grew up in a working class family (.) I wouldn't be standing here as First
>
> Minister of Scotland without the free education I had access to (.) as a politician
>
> now I have no right to take that same entitlement away from the next generation
>
> of young people

In this extract there is another reminder that Sturgeon is First Minister of Scotland. It is preceded, however, by an assertion that she was not brought up with the expectation of power: her achievements were made possible, in part, by the access working-class students of her generation had to state-funded higher education. In Extract 15, too, Sturgeon allies herself with 'ordinary people' rather than the privileged class to which the leaders of the main parties by implication belong, saying: '*their* priorities are wrong, but *they* won't pay the price; it will be *ordinary people* across the country who pay the price' (emphasis and punctuation added). Sturgeon is powerful, yet at the same time, she presents herself as 'ordinary', drawing an implicit contrast with the male leaders (who are all middle class and, with the exception of Miliband, privately educated), and addressing what politicians know is a common perception among voters, that the political class has little understanding of the people they purport to represent.

In Extract 15 there is also an 'us' to set against 'them': what we have labelled as point 2 is developed through a three-part list of policies 'none of us' can afford. The construction of Sturgeon and the audience as 'us' while the main party leaders are 'not-us' does not always rely on the explicit use of personal pronouns, however: in the comment we reproduced in Chap. 2 as Extract 9, Sturgeon uses a 'conducive' interrogative form (in this case, a tag question) which presupposes the audience's agreement, thus including them in the 'us' she is constructing, here specifically in opposition to the coalition leaders: 'it's ironic *isn't it* hearing Nick Clegg and David Cameron argue when they have been hand in glove imposing austerity on the people of this country for the last five years'. This inclusive address to the audience, combined with explicit references to her own ordinariness and her difference from the male leaders, helps Sturgeon to come across as confident but not arrogant, and to satisfy the popular demand for leaders who are 'authentic', real people with experience of real life.

This perception of Sturgeon is probably reinforced by the sound of her voice. Though a detailed analysis of the leaders' vocal performances is beyond the scope of this book, an obvious difference between the male and the female leaders is that all the women speak with noticeable localized accents—Australian for Bennett, Welsh for Wood, and Scots for Sturgeon—whereas all the men speak with variants of the educated English accent which is more a mark of class status than of place of origin. They are not all users of canonical Received Pronunciation (RP); Cameron is 'posher'-sounding than Miliband, for instance: the latter's accent includes a number of features of what is popularly called 'Estuary' English, such as relatively frequent final /t/ glottalization. However, these differences are less salient than the overarching difference between the men, whose accents index their membership of a privileged social group, and the women, whose accents index their ties to a particular part of the world. Research on attitudes to accents of English (e.g. Coupland and Bishop 2007) has repeatedly found that British informants judge speakers of non-localized, RP-like accents more positively than local-accented speakers for traits related to social status, such as authority, confidence, and intelligence, but less positively than local-accented speakers on measures related to social attractiveness, such as approachability, friendliness, sincerity, and trustworthiness. In some studies, 'cultured' Scots speakers (those whose local accents are mild or moderate rather than broad) have been positively rated on both sets of measures. It might be said, then, that Nicola Sturgeon had the perfect accent in which to project the desired combination of articulacy and authenticity to a UK-wide audience.

Accent, of course, is not usually the product of deliberate choice or calculation. But there are other aspects of her vocal performance which Sturgeon does control, such as variations in speech rate, loudness, pitch, and voice quality—for instance, the use she makes of a 'laughing voice' to signal irony during the comment that begins 'it's ironic, isn't it....' (Extract 9). As we noted in Chap. 2, Sturgeon is skilled in managing shifts in key, which is often done using the resources of body language, facial expression, prosody, and tone of voice, as well as by moving between different levels of formality. She is a dynamic performer who projects a range of affective stances, and this may also have helped to create the focus group members' impression of her as 'passionate' as well as 'strong'. Nigel Farage—the other leader who was judged to display both articulacy and authenticity—displayed a somewhat narrower linguistic and affective range. But the fact that he was perceived in a somewhat similar way to Sturgeon, though at first glance surprising, becomes more understandable in the light of the similarities the analysis reveals. Next, we reproduce his closing statement in the first debate, laid out in a similar way to Sturgeon's in Extract 15:

Extract 19

1. you see I warned you at the beginning I said they were all the same [laughter] what you've [laughter] an' what you've seen tonight is the politically correct political class

2. ooh they're very keen to be popular on the international stage

    a. they don't understand the (i) thoughts (ii) hopes and (iii) aspirations of ordinary people in this country

    b. they are detached

    c. most of them have never had a job in their lives er

3. what we represent is plain-spoken patriotism

    a. we believe in this country

    b. we believe in its people

    c. we believe Britain can be better than this

4. But if you want things to be shaken up and change properly you've gotta put more Ukip MPs in Westminster

    a. we won two by-elections last year

    b. we can outshine all expectations on May the seventh

5. let's do it

Farage may claim to represent 'plain-spoken patriotism', but he does not entirely reject the rhetorical tricks of the political speaker's trade. He avoids the appearance of artifice, however, by using markers of a casual, colloquial speech style (like 'you see', 'ooh', 'you've gotta...', 'let's do it'). Like Sturgeon, he designs his statement to address the negative perception of politicians as a privileged class who neither share nor understand the experiences of the voting public, and to identify himself and UKIP with the 'ordinary people of this country'. Farage, a privately educated former City broker, cannot claim he 'grew up in a working-class family', but his reference to 'the politically correct political class' is one of a number of comments in which he says or implies that he is an outsider, the only politician who dares to challenge orthodox wisdom on contentious issues like immigration. Like Sturgeon, he manipulates formality, tone, and key to change the footing of the interaction. In Extract 19, for instance, his informal, dialogic address to the audience at the beginning of his closing statement (which follows a much more formal, evidently pre-scripted statement by Natalie Bennett), realigns the relationship of speaker and audience in a semi-humorous, 'conspiratorial' way. In other sequences he breaks out of the ritualized conflict frame we expect in political debates, producing something that sounds more like a genuine outburst of anger and/or disbelief. As we saw in Chap. 2, at one point (Extract 7), he tells an opponent 'to stop LYING' (something that is expressly forbidden in the highly ritualized exchanges of Parliamentary debate), and there is also a point (Extract 8) where he vents his irritation by shouting 'can we GET REAL PLEASE'. These interventions typically prompt a response from the audience: the response is not always positive (when he accuses the studio audience in the BBC debate of left-wing bias, some audience members respond by booing), but it speaks to his ability to provoke a strong reaction. It also helps to explain why he, like Sturgeon, was seen by focus group members as 'authentic' (even where they were alienated by some of his political views).

At the beginning of this discussion, we said we would consider what role, if any, gender played in Nicola Sturgeon's performance. As we saw in Chap. 3, press coverage of the debates persistently foregrounded gender when discussing all the female party leaders, both individually and collectively. But it is striking that the women themselves did not refer to it at all during the debates. That was not because they avoided all kinds of personal talk about themselves: some aspects of personal identity and experience were mentioned by all the leaders, both male and female. There were, for instance, many references to national identity, both British and other—the two nationalists referred to their Scottishness and Welshness, Bennett spoke of her experiences as an immigrant, and Miliband spoke of being the child of immigrants. Clegg pointed out that he and Farage were both married to immigrants. There were also references to social class, some explicit, like Sturgeon's in Extract 18, others more oblique. But Sturgeon's reference to 'the old boys' network at Westminster' (p. 128), was the only explicit mention of any participant's gender in either debate. No speaker asserted that she/he spoke from their experience as a man or a woman, or addressed men or women as distinct subgroups of viewers. And although Winters and Carvalho's focus group findings have not yet been reported fully, their summary of focus group members' comments on the leaders does not mention anyone commenting on Sturgeon specifically as a female politician.

That is not to suggest that gender was not at some level a factor in her performance, or its reception by viewers: gender is, in both obvious and subtle ways, something all speakers are communicating all the time. Rather, we are suggesting that in the context of the debates, gender was in the background rather than the foreground. It was a taken-for-granted aspect of Sturgeon's performance rather than something she explicitly called attention to, and for the national television audience (as opposed to the media 'commentariat'), other aspects of the identity she performed may have played a more significant role in shaping their perceptions of her.

CONCLUSION

What we have presented in this book is a case study, focusing on the performances of a small number of individual politicians—and especially, of three female party leaders—in two debates that were broadcast on UK national television during the GE2015 campaign. We make no claim that Natalie Bennett, Nicola Sturgeon, and Leanne Wood are typical representatives of the category of female political speakers, let alone of female speakers more generally. On the contrary, they are clearly very untypical: while few individuals of either sex will ever address the nation as the leader of a political party, the number of women who have ever done this in the UK can be counted on the fingers of one hand. (Or two hands, if we include the other women apart from Sturgeon who have led their parties in Scotland, and the two who were generally treated, though contrary to their own preference for collectivism, as the leaders of the Northern Ireland Women's Coalition.)

But it is this lack of typicality that makes the three women interesting as a case study. The GE2015 debates were a rare case in which men and women who held the same institutional role (party leader) participated in the same political speech events, in close to equal numbers (four men and three women in one debate, two men and three women in the other), under conditions in which they were all subject to the same rules, and treated, if not quite equally (the leaders of major parties, all of them male, had certain advantages), then at least with notional parity of esteem. We set out to investigate how female politicians actually used language under those conditions, and in particular whether they differed from their male counterparts in the ways suggested by expert and popular discourse on language, gender, and politics. We also considered how the reception and media representation of their performances related to our analysis of the performances themselves, and to what extent it was influenced by ideological preconceptions about women's 'different voice'.

On the first of these questions, we concluded that the linguistic behaviour of the men and women who participated in the debates did not display clear-cut, and clearly gender-based, differences. There were some patterns which were linked to gender, such as the overall tendency for men to take more speaking time, but in our view, these were most directly related to other variables, such as the status of a leader as either an incumbent or a challenger, and among the challengers, his or her status as the leader of a major or a minor party. The most noticeable stylistic differences were between individuals, and intra-gender differences were no less striking than inter-gender ones. Cameron and Farage, for example, had very different debating styles, and so did Sturgeon and Bennett. In the latter case, the very considerable difference between the two women is most readily explained in terms of Sturgeon's much more extensive political experience.

On the second question, we concluded that the 'different voice' ideology remains a powerful influence on the representation of women in politics. We also noted that women's supposedly distinctive style of communication is most commonly represented—by commentators across the political spectrum—in positive rather than negative (or neutral) terms; with few exceptions, 'the women' were praised for their contribution to civilizing political discourse. As Clare Walsh (2001) has noted, though, the idea that women have a mission, or even an obligation, to civilize men's discourse, or the institutions men dominate, is as much of a constraint on women as it is an opportunity for them. It reinforces the existing, narrow definition of 'acceptable' female behaviour, and forces individual women who do not conform to, or wish to be limited by, that definition to engage in complicated forms of (in Janet Holmes's phrase) 'impression management' in an effort to ensure they are neither dismissed as insufficiently authoritative nor derided as aggressive 'battleaxes'. The most experienced and skilful of the three women in our case study, Nicola Sturgeon, did not entirely escape the second of these negative outcomes, though some evidence (from opinion polls and focus group research) suggests that the attacks made on her by the right-wing English press may not have reflected, or had much influence on, the perceptions of the public that watched the debates themselves.

In both linguistics and politics, an argument commonly made by advocates of the 'different voice' account of language and gender (e.g. Tannen 1990; Karpowitz and Mendelberg 2014) is that women should not have to behave exactly like men to be treated as men's equals. We agree: like other scholars who take a critical perspective on the relationship between language and gender (e.g. Baxter 2014; Walsh 2001), we do not wish to deny the value of what is conventionally thought of as a 'female' way of speaking. What we are critical of is the ideology which suggests that this style 'comes naturally' to women. On the one hand, that suggestion gives women no credit for making principled decisions about how to communicate (or for the skills they display when they do so); on the other, it may imply that other styles are not legitimate choices for female speakers. We are also uneasy about the implications of some 'different voice' arguments which focus specifically on women's position in political institutions: at the extreme, these can appear to be suggesting that the main reason we should want women to be better represented is *because* they are different from men, and that if women simply duplicated men's concerns or their behaviour, there would be less reason for concern about their under-representation. Insisting that women must be different from men is no better than demanding they be the same. Women deserve equal political representation simply because, like men, they are people.

The styles of speaking which the 'different voice' ideology genders— 'male' adversarial styles and 'female' consensus-based styles—both have important functions in democratic political discourse, and even in the primarily adversarial genre of the debate, we see elements of both being used, by both male and female politicians. The cause of women's political equality would be advanced, we believe, if instead of praising the civilizing influence of women's 'different voice', we acknowledged that the most effective political speakers, male and female, are those who use a range of linguistic resources to construct a voice of their own.

REFERENCES

Atkinson, M. (1984). *Our masters' voices: The language and body language of politics*. London: Methuen.

Baxter, J. (2010). *The language of female leadership*. London; New York, NY: Palgrave Macmillan.

Baxter, J. (2011). Survival or success? A critical exploration of the use of 'double-voiced discourse' by women business leaders in the UK. *Discourse & Communication, 5*(3), 231–245.

Baxter, J. (2014). *Double-voicing at work: Power, gender and linguistic expertise*. Basingstoke: Palgrave Macmillan.

Bell, A. (1984). Language style as audience design. *Language in Society, 13*(2), 145–204.

Cammaerts, B. (2015). Did Britain's right-wing newspapers win it for the Tories? *LSE GE2015*, May 13 [online]. http://blogs.lse.ac.uk/generalelection/is-it-the-daily-hate-co-wot-won-it/. Accessed 26 September 2015.

Coupland, N., & Bishop, H. (2007). Ideologised values for British accents. *Journal of Sociolinguistics, 11*(1), 74–93.

Edelsky, C., & Adams, K. (1990). Creating inequality: Breaking the rules in debates. *Journal of Language and Social Psychology, 9*(3), 171–190.

Holmes, J. (2006). *Gendered talk in the workplace*. Oxford: Blackwell.

Karpowitz, C., & Mendelberg, T. (2014). *The silent sex*. Princeton: Princeton University Press.

McDowell, J. (2015). Masculinity and non-traditional occupations: Men's talk in women's work, *Gender. Work & Organization, 22*(3), 273–291.

McElhinny, B. (1995). Challenging hegemonic masculinities: Female and male police officers handling domestic violence. In K. Hall & M. Buchholtz (Eds.), *Gender articulated: Language and the socially constructed self* (pp. 217–244). New York: Routledge.

Shaw, S. (2006). Governed by the rules? The female voice in Parliamentary debates. In J. Baxter (Ed.), *Speaking out: The female voice in public contexts* (pp. 81–102). Basingstoke: Palgrave Macmillan.

Tannen, D. (1990). *You just don't understand: Men and women in conversation*. New York: Ballantine.

TNS Global. (2015). Nicola Sturgeon tops the approval ratings for leaders' performance. 29 April [online]. http://www.tnsglobal.com/uk/press-release/nicola-sturgeon-tops-ratings-for-leaders-performance. Accessed 29 September 2015.

Walsh, C. (2001). *Gender and discourse: Language and power in politics, the church and institutions.* London: Longman.

Winters, K., & Carvalho, E. (2015). Why did Nicola and Nigel do so well out of the debates? They are authentic and articulate, that's why. QESB 2015, 3 May [online]. https://wintersresearch.wordpress.com/media-coverage/blog-articles/. Accessed 29 September 2015.

Index

137

Printed by Printforce, the Netherlands